MW00580392

The Image of the Puppet in Italian Theater, Literature and Film

"Due to its originality and expressive variety, the puppet theater in Italy represents a unique phenomenon that cannot be found in any other Western country. However, in the face of such extraordinary richness, there are still very few scholarly studies on the subject, even though some efforts have been made to fill the void through essays, exhibitions, and the opening of various museums in recent years. In his book contribution, Federico Pacchioni delves into the world of animated figures with an entirely personal curiosity and an original slant, investigating the metaphorical perception of puppets, their function in terms of the fantastic stimulation of a shared memory capable of recalling the naivete of childhood as well as developing purely philosophical notions. The author combines scientific rigor with a literary vein that, besides making the reading of the study very pleasant, allows him to propose novel connections, to suggest possible affinities and elements of reflection on the vitality and evocative power of puppet theater."

—Alfonso Cipolla, *Professor of Theater at the Conservatory G. Cantelli; Director of the Institute of Marionette Culture and Popular Theater of Grugliasco, Turin, Italy*

Federico Pacchioni

The Image
of the Puppet
in Italian Theater,
Literature and Film

palgrave
macmillan

Federico Pacchioni
Chapman University
Orange, CA, USA

ISBN 978-3-030-98667-4   ISBN 978-3-030-98668-1   (eBook)
https://doi.org/10.1007/978-3-030-98668-1

ABOUT THIS BOOK

This book was first published in Italian language by Metauro Editore (2020). Some of the chapters rework research previously published in article form in journals and volumes: *The Passion of a Puppet: Rebranded Wooden Heads in the Shadow of Commedia dell'Arte,* "Intersections. Review of the History of Ideas" 3 (2009), pp. 339–356; *Vulgarity and Grace: Lina Wertmüller's Figure Cinema,* "L'ANELLO che non tiene: Journal of Modern Italian Literature", 24.12 (2012), pp. 147–160; *La contaminazione tra teatro di figura e cinema in* Cosa sono le nuvole?, in Simona Wright and Fulvio Orsitto (eds.), *Contaminazioni culturali. Music, theater, cinema and literature in contemporary Italy,* Rome, Vecchiarelli, 2014, pp. 233–244; Novecento *tra poesia e politica: Bertolucci e il teatro popolare dei burattini,* in "Rivista Luci e Ombre. Quarterly of film and cultural information" 4.1 (April–June 2016), rivist alucieombre.com; *Il pupo emigrato: dal teatro allo schermo,* in "Italian Canadiana" vol. 31 (2017), pp. 155–164; *Lo schermo e il burattino: intermediality and remediation between figure theater and silent cinema,* "California Italian Studies Journal," vol. 7.1 (2017), escholarship.org.

CONTENTS

LIST OF FIGURES

CHAPTER 1

Introduction

Abstract The introductory chapter presents the author's direct experience with puppetry in Italy and the book's scholarly aim. Four types of traditional puppet theater are introduced: the commedia dell'arte glove puppet (*burattino*), the Northern string marionette (*marionetta*), the Southern older marionette (*opera dei pupi*) and the Neapolitan Pulcinella puppet (*teatro delle guarattelle*). This chapter introduces critical notions that highlight the psychological and cultural saliency of the puppet as both an object and an idea or image. The integration of cultural history and artistic texts is discussed and presented along with an overview of the twentieth-century Italian writers, painters, and filmmakers at the center of the book's analysis.

Keywords Italian puppet theater · Italian puppetry · Burattino · Marionetta · Pupo · Pulcinella · Pinocchio · Twentieth century · Italian literature and cinema · Mask · Self · Avatar · Simulacrum · Identity · Realism

I remember the day I first returned to Italy after moving to the United States: I walked down the stairs to my father's study in the damp, cool basement, and I began to rummage through the single trunk containing the remnants of a puppet theater that had been sold. All I found inside

F. Pacchioni, *The Image of the Puppet in Italian Theater, Literature and Film*, https://doi.org/10.1007/978-3-030-98668-1_1

the trunk was a half-sculpted wooden head, and two pairs of hands, a pack of *canovacci*, and, at the bottom, collections of wrinkled *lazzi*,[1] but the familiar smell of paint and formaldehyde, the roughness of that simulated flesh, and the wink of that barely discernible face were enough to make me feel as if I were surrounded again by the warmth of the old puppet theater.

When I was a child, my father, a professor at the conservatory of Bologna and a lover of the popular arts of his land, would don the hat of street artist during summer break. After a period of apprenticeship with a puppeteer from Modena and various experiences as a bagpiper or with puppets accompanied by ocarinas that he used to make himself, my father took his company of Emilian-style glove puppets from *Il Teatro di Fagiolino* on tour around Europe in a white Fiat bus.

At the time, with my small arms, I could not yet hold the puppets with their bulky, heavy heads—characteristic of the theaters of the Po Valley— as my older brother could, which limited my role in operating the stereo, opening and closing the curtain, and changing backdrops. My moments of glory came from creating the special effects: blowing into the pipe full of sulfur powder with a lighted candle on top to make the flame blaze at the command of the magician or devil or squeezing the water pump behind the proscenium when Fagiolino or Sandrone could no longer hold it—all to the great delight of the public.

I particularly remember my father's satisfaction when he worked for a year in the permanent theater of a small town in Romagna. The clois- tered and distraction-free environment of the theater gave prominence to the shows and helped the puppeteer to concentrate, which did not happen at the more chaotic Festival dell'Unità or in the schools or the shopping malls where we were sometimes called. We also performed in other contexts, such as town fairs and folk-art festivals, along with other performances of various kinds, Italian or otherwise.

During these festivals, I observed with my young eyes the shows of puppeteers now considered historical figures; I admired the bewil- dering puppets of Otello Sarzi (1922–2001), abandoned myself to the exhilarating and unstoppable logic of Gaspare Nasuto's *guarattelle* (1972–), contemplated the exploits of Mimmo Cuticchio's *pupi* (1948–),

---

[1] The terms *canovacci* and *lazzi* respectively relate to the scenarios and the stock comedic routines of commedia dell'arte, the widely influential Italian Renaissance form of popular theater at the base of much of Italian puppetry.

and shared my father's enthusiasm for the best demonstrations of the
commedia dell'arte *burattini*, among which always loomed large the
brilliant intelligence of Romano Danielli (1937–), the colorful and up-
to-date spectacles of the Ferrari family, and the surprising scenographic
inventions of Erio Maletti (1932–2011).[2]

It is, therefore, no accident that respect for the puppet's magic—
that complex wonder so evident to the eyes of a child—has inspired the
creation of this book. Moreover, as the work of an expatriate author, this
study corresponds to a return, a desire to fill once again that trunk found
half-empty in the cellar of a childhood home. However, as often happens
when digging into one's past, one inevitably finds precious elements
that go beyond the intimate sphere and reorder threads of larger stories
through cross-cultural and artistic spheres.

The enchantment underlying the exceptional psychological, cultural,
and aesthetic values of the puppet is linked to that of the mask in the
archaic rituals observed in numerous cultures, in which the mask implies a
"transformation of self into another 'I,'" as noted by the German ethno-
grapher Oskar Eberle,[3] or the creation of "a living amalgam" between
the self and the potential life of the object, as concluded by scholar
and theater artist John Emigh.[4] This dialogic projection of the self into
the inanimate is a purely human capacity, founded in the animistic and
fetishistic thinking that characterizes not only so-called primitive cultures
but also modern humans, as revealed by Victoria Nelson's reflections on

[2] It is helpful to specify the meaning of some basic terms at the outset. Often *puppet*
and *marionette* are used as synonyms to refer to animated puppets in general, but in
this study, I use them in their specific sense when needed. The puppet (or *burattino*) is
controlled from below through a glove, while the marionette (or *marionetta*) is controlled
from above using wires. Furthermore, the *pupo* is a marionette typical of the south
of the peninsula, operated by rods and a few strings, while *guarattelle* theater involves
the Neapolitan Pulcinella glove puppet, which is generally characterized by a smaller
wooden head in contrast to that of the northern glove puppets of the Po Valley. With
the expressions *theater of animation* and *puppet theater*, I refer to all of the above forms
of puppetry (as well as to object theater).

[3] Oskar Eberle, *Cenalora: Vita, religione, danza, teatro dei popoli primitivi* (Milan: Il
Saggiatore, 1966), 608. Throughout this book, translations are mine unless otherwise
indicated.

[4] John Emigh, *Masked Performance: The Play of Self and Other in Ritual and Theater*
(Philadelphia: University of Pennsylvania Press, 1996), 275.

the cult of the simulacrum in the imaginary of mass culture,[5] or the reflections on the new fetish of money and technology in Alf Hornborg's eco-anthropological criticism.[6]

It is not so rash to affirm that today we find ourselves in the era of the puppet: we are more and more willing and accustomed to suspend our critical sense and to live through simulacra of the ego (multiple virtual profiles and avatars) and to identify ourselves with them, although they are obvious embodiments of social fiction, and we become, in adopting them, increasingly chained to the struggle to defend our own image and reputation, to what a famous Pirandellian character recognizes as the "war of the puppets."[7] Paradoxically, however, we know little of the puppet's history or even of the puppet itself. Accordingly, examining works of art steeped into the idea of the puppet and its implications can be particularly useful and relevant today.

The puppet object implies a stance on oneself as well as on the human condition that is, in general, both historical and spiritual. As will be shown in the following pages, such awareness occurs not only relative to the puppet as a theatrical object but also relative to the puppet as an image or an idea. To acquire a deeper understanding of the specific interpretations of human existence for which the puppet often becomes a vehicle, my study follows the life of the puppet image offstage and within various artistic fields.

The great richness and variety of puppet theater in Italy makes the national context an ideal analytical framework for the study of the idea of the puppet. The different forms of puppet theater are at the root of specific evocations and discourses that in turn inspire a vast horizon of inventions, interpretations, and intermedial phenomena. Even when

[5] Victoria Nelson, *The Secret Life of Puppets* (Cambridge, MA: Harvard University Press, 2001).

[6] See for example Alf Hornborg, "Knowledge of Persons, Knowledge of Things: Animism, Fetishism, and Objectivism as Strategies for Knowing (or not Knowing) the World," *Ethos* 71, no. 1 (2006): 1–12; Alf Hornborg, "The Political Economy of Technofetishism," *Journal of Ethnographic Theory* 5, no. 1 (2015): 1–17.

[7] The image comes from *Il berretto a sonagli—Comedy in Two Acts* by Luigi Pirandello, where the metaphor of the *pupo* is used extensively. The comedy, written in August 1916 in Sicilian dialect with the title *'A birritta cu' i ciancianeddi* and represented for the first time at the Teatro Nazionale in Rome on June 27, 1917, was then rewritten by Pirandello in an Italian version. This standard edition is *Il berretto a rattagli / La giara / Il piacere dell'onestà*, ed. R. Alonge (Milan: Arnoldo Mondadori, 1992).

the references to puppets in literature and cinema have a documentary quality, situating themselves precisely in the context of Italian political and theatrical history, the references nonetheless repurpose the puppet as a metaphor, thus inflecting at the same time its deeper values and meanings.

In opening this book, the theater historian may have doubts about the value of investigating the idea of the puppet through literary and filmic interpretations, fearing that such research will merely repeat representational stereotypes and myths without doing justice to the complexity and variety of theatrical practices. In part, this danger is curbed by the realistic vein of many of the observed texts, especially certain films. More importantly, I will be examining artistic interpretations critically in terms of the aesthetic and cultural peculiarities of the theatrical traditions to which they refer. To go beyond the stereotyped view of the puppet is, in fact, my study's primary goal. I aim to situate my work at the intersections of fields such as: history of ideas, literary and theater history, film history, and textual interpretation; and, in so doing, reveal the subtle, unprecedented functions that the Italian puppet theater has in a broad artistic and cross-cultural context.

The choice of not devoting a chapter entirely to Pinocchio supports my goal of examining the idea of the puppet outside the overbearing shadow of this fascinating character and the totemic function it typically plays in canonical literature about puppets. Because he is both a *burattino* and a *marionetta* and takes myriad forms in numerous literary, theatrical, and cinematic adaptations, Pinocchio is a continent to which we will return often in this book, reevaluating its boundaries and identifying new areas of significance. However, by highlighting the cultural life of puppetry in a broader sense, one can better appreciate Pinocchio's theatrical dimensions and the fact that this best-known fable is only the tip of the puppetry iceberg.

Tracing the evolution of the puppet metaphor means following its emergence in historically and artistically distant moments to grasp its functions and broader meaning. Thus, my analysis interweaves examples from the works of quite diverse artists, among whom writers such as Luigi Pirandello (1867–1936), Filippo Tommaso Marinetti (1876–1944), and Massimo Bontempelli (1878–1960); painters such as Giorgio de Chirico (1888–1978); and especially directors such as Roberto Rossellini (1906–1977), Vittorio De Sica (1901–1974), Federico Fellini (1920–1993), Pier Paolo Pasolini (1922–1975), Bernardo Bertolucci (1941–2018), and Lina Wertmüller (1928–2021). The wealth of multifaceted references to puppets in the work of these artists undoubtedly reflects the fact that these men and women of the twentieth century grew up in contact with puppet theater when it was still part of everyday life. As this study hopes to demonstrate, their work can serve as a bridge, not only for preserving the tradition but also for showing its strength and continued vitality within other media.

It is, in fact, thanks to the complex process of transformation and reinterpretation into image or idea that the puppet continues to live in a significant way; understanding this process of renewal and evolution is at the heart of my research. Specifically, I will examine the historical and cultural implications of intermedial interpretation not only in relation to the history of literature and cinema but also in relation to authorial contexts and artistic currents. If the perspective of remediation reveals dynamics of rivalry, among which those occurring between cinema and puppet theater stand out, my examination of stylistic choices and collaboration illuminates the meanings of artists' creative decisions.

The order of the texts studied here does not follow a rigid chronology; rather, the book is organized as a spiral in which the chapters overlap, returning to and reframing historical periods and artistic movements. In addition, although I focus on the theme of the puppet in the Italian context, I also take stock of a broader international panorama, by following an identity thread in Italian American cinema. Finally, the study of the intermedial life of the puppet offers a clear illustration of how older forms of entertainment reveal themselves to be part of a genealogy—sometimes explicit and sometimes concealed—that generates and stimulates modern and contemporary cultural production, including the animated film.

This book is inspired by the work of all the puppeteers I have been fortunate to observe at work over the years, who, with their talent, wisdom, and humanity, have ensured that the fascination with the puppet be deeply rooted in me. First and foremost, my father, Giorgio Pacchioni, who, thanks to his curiosity about the world of folklore, filled my childhood with memorable and precious experiences. The performances of many artists, including those still active mentioned at the beginning of this introduction have been and continue to be a source of wonder and inspiration. I must thank all those who have supported various aspects of my research by sharing impressions, suggestions, and materials, especially: Laura di Bianco, Alfonso Cipolla, Helen De Michiel, Stefano Giunchi, Michele Guerra, Millicent Marcus,

Mauro Monticelli, Domenico Napoletani, Paolo Parmiggiani, and John Welle. The analysis of many films central to this research would not have been possible without the archives of the Museo Nazionale del Cinema di Torino, the archives of the Castello dei Burattini-Museo Giordano Ferrari of Parma, the Cineteca of Bologna, the Cineteca del Friuli and the Centro Regionale per l'Inventario e la Catalogazione-Filmoteca Regionale Siciliana. Finally, I would like to express my gratitude to Chapman University, which has provided me with a stimulating intellectual community over the years that accompanied my exploration of the themes and cases contained in this book: from the amicable support of colleagues from The Puppet Metaphor Research Group (Wendy Salmon, Polly Hodge, Pia Bazhaf, and Georgia Panteli) to the attentive students in my course The Puppet Metaphor Across Media. Also at Chapman University, I would also like to thank Leatherby Libraries and its staff for their assistance, Provost Glenn Pfeiffer for granting me the sabbatical needed to compile the book, and Marybelle and Paul Musco for their generous and ongoing support.

CHAPTER 2

Burattino, a Name and an Idea: From Commedia dell'Arte to Pinocchio

Abstract This chapter describes the historical and semantic process by which the commedia dell'arte character of Burattino gave its name to Italian puppets (burattini). This discussion analyzes Burattino's mechanical performative qualities, which were hinted at in late Renaissance scenarios by Flaminio Scala and Francesco Gattici, as well as the dominant themes of misfortune and victimization often connected to this character; by doing so, it reveals the full significance of the naming of the puppets. The Burattino-like identity of Italian puppets is also traced in specific narrative passages contained in Collodi's *Pinocchio*.

Keywords Italian literature · Italian Renaissance theater · Commedia dell'arte · Censorship · Charlatans · Burattino · *Canovacci* · Scenarios · Flaminio Scala · Carlo de Vecchi · Francesco Gattici · Marginalization · Pinocchio

The roots of puppet theater are ancient and go back to stone idols, Greek mechanical statues, sacred representations, and medieval and Renaissance mechanical devices, expressions of the incarnation of the sacred and the search for wonder. In Europe, in the late Middle Ages and during the

F. Pacchioni, *The Image of the Puppet in Italian Theater, Literature and Film*, https://doi.org/10.1007/978-3-030-98668-1_2

entire Renaissance, puppets and marionettes were part of street attractions often seen as the cunning activities of wanderers, barkers, and acrobats. As engravings from the sixteenth and seventeenth centuries demonstrate, various types of spectacles alternated and mixed on stages in city squares. It was not out of the ordinary for the street artist to pass from a performance as an actor to one as a puppeteer.

Examining the reciprocal influences between puppet theater and actors' theater, whether in competition or cooperation, we immediately come across a suggestive coincidence of names and dates between the appearance of the commedia dell'arte mask of Burattino and, upon its gradual disappearance, the almost immediate labeling of the street artists' puppets as *burattini*.[1] This coincidence offers an opportunity to reflect on the relationship between puppet theater and actors' theater and to define fundamental qualities of the idea of puppetry in Italy, following traces and clues in the city squares of the late sixteenth century up to the nineteenth-century threshold of Pinocchio.

Based on etymological data, we know that in Medieval Vulgar Latin, *buratinus* signified the flour sifter, who took his name from his work tool, his sieve, that is, the *buratto*, an instrument in turn named for the

---

[1] Since the nineteenth century, numerous historians have noted the change of name without, however, analyzing its cultural significance. I refer to the studies of Charles Magnin, Maurice Sand, and Louis Moland. Consider this passage: "At a remote time, and it would be reckless for a foreigner to want to specify too much, the favorite character, the hero of the puppets of Italy was a famous mask of the commedia dell'arte, Roman or Florentine of origin, called *Burattino*. This character acquired such great fame that he was admitted to puppet theaters, which were called *burattini* after him." See Charles Magnin, *Histoire des marionnettes en Europe: Depuis l'antiquité jusqu'a nos jours* (Paris: Michel Lévy Frères, 1852), 86. Another such passage is "In 1550, in Italy, they were called *bagatelli* and *magatelli*; but Burattino, one of the masks of Italian comedy, had personified himself in the marionettes and his name remained with those that were generally called *burattini* from the end of the sixteenth century onward." See Maurice Sand, *Masques et bouffons (comédie italienne): Texte et dessins* (Paris: Michel Lévy Frères, 1860), 30. Taking a different position, the scholar Yorick son of Yorick (alias of Pietro Coccoluto Ferrigni) argued, in his *Storia dei burattini* (Florence: Bemporad, 1902), that the mask (meaning here a type character) was so named because it resembled a puppet. For a more in-depth discussion of the debate regarding the origin of the name *burattino* and the reasons that lead me to support the hypothesis that the mask was the starting point, see the more extensive philological analysis: Federico Pacchioni, "La passione di un Burattino: Teste di legno ribattezzate all'ombra della Commedia dell'Arte," *Intersezioni. Rivista di storia delle idee* 3 (2009): 339–356.

bura of which it was made, a sparse and coarse mesh.[2] As is usual with the types of the commedia dell'arte, even that of Burattino was probably a parody of a certain social class: the humble sifter, perhaps particularly comical because of the tedious and mechanical humiliation to which his work subjects him, his being always after flour but nevertheless poor and hungry.

The fact that Burattino's persona featured accentuated characteristics of *zanni* (the commedia dell'arte servant type) in its gestures and ignorance may have contributed to what today we understand as a meta-representative predisposition, a caricature, and stylization of the *zanni* type itself. Perhaps because of this typological transparency, in 1615, Camillo Conti da Panico imagined Burattino sending a sonnet of greeting and good wishes to all the *zanni* leaving for the Land of Cuccagna at the end of Carnival.[3] Therefore, *burattini* appear as the most explicit reflection of the archetypal and caricatural core of the *zanni*. Thus, at the beginning of the seventeenth century, the first occurrences of a passage using the word *burattino* were recorded.[4] It remains to be seen, nonetheless, what this shift implies for the history of the Italian idea of the puppet,

[2] For etymological sources see Giacomo Devoto, *Avviamento alla etimologia italiana: Dizionario etimologico* (Florence: Mondadori, 1979); Salvatore Battaglia, *Grande dizionario della lingua italiana* (Turin: UTET, 1961); Tullio De Mauro, *Grande dizionario italiano dell'uso* (Turin: UTET, 1999).

[3] Camillo Conti da Panico, "Daspuò che al Carneval vol andar via," in *La commedia dell'Arte: Storia e testi*, ed. Vito Pandolfi (Florence: Edizioni Sansoni Antiquariato, 1957), 4:3637.

[4] In the heroicomic poem *Malmantile racquistato* by Lorenzo Lippi (1606–1664), we find puppets as entertainment alongside the *zanni*: "L'andar il giorno in piazza a'burattini / Ed agli Zanni, furon le loro gite" ("Their outings consisted of going to the piazza to see puppets and Zannis") See Lorenzo Lippi, *Malmantile racquistato* (Florence: Stamperia di G. T. Rossi, 1676), 34 (cantare II, strofa XLVI). Useful for identifying the type of theater in question is a note in the commentary to the poem: "He means those wooden puppets [*figurini*], which are moved by one who to such effect hides in a wooden structure covered with cloth [*castelletto*], and operates them by putting them on the tips of his fingers, and with a certain whistle [*pivetta*] makes them speak." The commentary is by Paolo Minucci and appears in the 1688 edition of *Malmantile* by the Stamperia di Sua Maestà Serenissima alla Condotta in Florence. The most important and perhaps the first occurrence is, however, in the treatise of the theologian Domenico Ottonelli: "To this end some appear above a bench and show themselves inside a fake castle of cloth. *Giocalatori* [jugglers] with various puppets called *Burattini*, that is, little figures through which they make gestures and say words of great effectiveness, to excite delight and laughter in the spectators." See Domenico Ottonelli, *Della Christiana moderazione del Theatro: Detto la qualità delle Commedie* (Florence: Antonio Bonari, 1652), 436.

a dimension that can be accessed by removing the mask of Burattino from the shadow that still surrounds it.

Burattino makes his appearance among the masks of the second *zanni* of the Compagnia dei Gelosi (Company of the Jealous) between Pedrolino and Arlecchino.[5] Under the direction of Flaminio Scala, with leading actors such as Francesco and Isabella Andreini, the Compagnia dei Gelosi was formed in Milan in 1568 and then dissolved upon the death of Isabella in 1604. Her son, Giovan Battista Andreini (also known as Lelio), continued the family tradition within the company of the Duke of Mantua, directed by Pier Maria Cecchini (Frittellino) from 1605 to 1609. The Mantuan context is important because, as revealed by Andreini's and Cecchini's correspondence, the part of Burattino was then played by Carlo de Vecchi (?–1609). In 1609, when the disagreements between Cecchini and his wife, Flaminia, on the one hand, and between Andreini and the actors of the company, on the other, became more acute, De Vecchi was killed by the Cecchini couple. This sensational murder may have contributed to associating the name of Burattino with a halo of misfortune and disgrace, to which must be added a certain alienation from reality and marginalization from social relations.[6]

The poet Giambattista Marino (1569–1625), who had probably met De Vecchi in Turin in 1609, mentions Burattino in a burlesque letter dated 1615 as an example of the clumsy servant who is incapable of assisting his master.[7] A little later, in mentioning the character's uniform, Tomaso Garzoni speaks of a "a swindler's little hat" and a "porter's

---

[5] Sand, *Masques et bouffons*, 258.

[6] This information derives from two letters of G. B. Andreini to Ferdinando Gonzaga (dated, respectively, August 13 and 14, 1609) and from a letter of P. M. Cecchini to Vincenzo I. Gonzaga (dated February 15, 1602), both of which can be consulted in *Comici dell'Arte: Corrispondenze*, ed. Claudia Burattelli, Domenica Landolfi, and Anna Zinanni (Florence: Le Lettere, 1993), 1:88–93, 115–16, 203–204, 210.

[7] "It happened that a scoundrel of a worker of the tavern who was trying to get me on a horse, not knowing that my rear end was in such bad shape because of the many bruises and the very little fat that was left there, and having grabbed me from below, looked like Burattino when he wants to dress up Pantalone; he threw me into the saddle in such a rude manner that, making me give a jolt, he almost had one of the family jewels crushed." See Giambattista Marino, *Lettere*, ed. Marziano Guglielminetti (Turin: Giulio Einaudi, 1966), 549. The meeting between Vecchi and Marino can be deduced from a letter of G. B. Andreini dated 1609, in which he mentions some polemical verses that Marino would have written about the scandalous and haughty behavior of Flaminia, Cecchini's wife, in Turin. See *Comici dell'Arte: Corrispondenze*, 1:90–91.

sack," placing an emphasis on the boorish nature of the character: "a Burattino who does not know how to do anything else than putting his little hat on his head."[8] In fact, in the famous *canovaccio* of the *Pazzia di Isabella* [Isabella's Madness], Burattino is the incapable servant who, perfectly useless to his masters, never knows how to answer their questions: "Pantalone asks him if he knows the reason why Orazio does not marry Isabella. Burattino: says that he does not know"; "Flaminia asks him if Horace is wounded. Burattino: says that he does not know"; and, again, "Pantalone asks him how long Isabella has been missing from home. Burattino: he doesn't know."[9]

Burattino appears in twenty of Scala's fifty plays, where his characteristic stupidity, that is, his alienation from reality and from the community, is evoked in numerous episodes, joining other typical characteristics of the figure of the servant in sixteenth-century comedy, notably lasciviousness and greed.[10] The French historian Louis Moland was the first to define the peculiarities of Scala's version of the character:

Also notable within the Scala troupe was the famous jester Burattino, who gave his name to all Italian puppets, which are still called *burattini*. Burattino played the role of the grumpy, clumsy servant, but more often

---

[8] Tomaso Garzoni, *La piazza universale di tutte le professioni del mondo*, ed. Paolo Cherchi and Beatrice Collina (1585; repr., Turin: Giulio Einaudi, 1996), 2:1184, 1193.

[9] The *canovaccio* is taken from Flaminio Scala, *Il teatro delle favole rappresentative* [Theater of Representative Fables, henceforth *Il teatro delle favole*], ed. Ferruccio Marotti (Milan: Edizioni Il Polifilo, 1976), 385–96. Among the earliest documents attesting to the presence of Burattino among the Gelosi is Giuseppe Pavironi's enthusiastic account of the staging of *La Pazzia di Isabella* on the occasion of the wedding between Ferdinando de' Medici and Cristina of Lorraine on May 3, 1589, in Florence. See *Don Ferdinando Medici and Sig. Donna Cristina di Lorena Gran Duchi di Toscana* in Scala, *Teatro delle favole*, LXXIII–LXXXV.

[10] The appearances of Burattino in the scenarios of *Della scena de soggetti comici e tragici* collected between 1618 and 1622 by the Roman academic and comic amateur Basilio Locatelli are numerous. Here are a few titles for which Pandolfi offers dialogues and synopses: *Li sei contenti, Li ritratti, Il veneno, Il Principe d'Altavilla, Le teste incantate, Le grandezze di Zanni, L'abbattimento di Zanni, Trappolini invisibile, La acconcia serve, Li spiriti, Lo amante ingrato, Li due simili di Plauto, Li tre schiavi, Li finti turchi, Il finto marito, Li finti amici, Le finte morte, Elijsa Alij Bassà, Proteo, La gelosia, La inimicitia, L'Intronati, Li tre matti, La trapolaria, La tuchetta, La zinghera, Li incanti amorosi, Il gran Mago, Il finto astrologo*, and *Amor costante*. See Pandolfi, *La commedia dell'Arte*, 5:223–252. For a complete list of the appearances of Burattino in scenarios by various authors, see Pacchioni, *La passione di un Burattino*, 346n27, 348n31, 350n38, 351n40, 452n44.

the messenger, the innkeeper, and the gardener. When a name is added to that of Burattino, it is the not-so-honest name of *Canaglia* [Rascal]. Husband of Franceschina and father of Olivette, he is generally unfortunate, deceived, and cheated and is sometimes seized with marked envy and a desire to deceive and defraud others. He is adept at all the jokes, often occupies the stage, and normally the roles he plays do not matter in the unfolding of the plot.[11]

He is, therefore, an ornamental background character, strongly typified, whose most frequent role, even outside the scenarios of the Scala troupe, remains that of the second *zanni*, an unfortunate and clumsy servant.[12] In the recurring episodes of amorous rivalry with Pedrolino for the attention of the servant Franceschina, Burattino is almost always the loser.[13] When he is finally married to Franceschina, he finds himself at the center of a series of deceptions and betrayals by her and other characters who try to "farlo un becco" (to make a cuckold out of him).[14] Within the wide panorama of misfortunes that the mask of Burattino encounters as the second *zanni*, the instances where he plays aggressive and powerful roles appear to involve something like revenge; here, he fully embodies the title of "Burattino Canaglia."[15]

Scala's scenarios *La fortuna di Flavio* [Flavio's Fortune], *Flavio finto negromante* [Flavio False Necromancer], *Il portalettere* [The Messenger], and *La mancata fede* [The Neglected Promise] are the ones where Burattino plays the most prominent roles. Among them, *La mancata fede* is particularly interesting in that it indicates some of the performative traits of his character. We encounter once again the incapable servant: "Burattino: at the window, half asleep. Pantalone asks him if Horace is at home. He: does not know."[16] Burattino soon falls into a complex

[11] Louis Moland, *La comédie italienne* (Paris: Didier Libraires, 1867), 53.

[12] This role can be found in the following plays by Scala: *La pazzia di Isabella*, *La fortuna di Isabella*, *Le disgrazie di Flavio*, *Flavio finto negromante*, *Il pedante*, *Li tre fidi amici*, *Il portalettere*, *Il finto cieco*, *Il creduto morto*, *La mancata fede*, and *Il finto cieco*.

[13] See Scala's scenarios *Il portalettere*, *Il finto cieco*, *Le disgrazie di Flavio*, and *La fortuna di Isabella*.

[14] Scala, *Teatro delle favole*, 60. See also *Flaminio finto negromante* and *Le burle di Isabella*.

[15] See *Caccia*, in Scala, *Teatro delle favole*, 375. "Burattino Canaglia" will also return in the sonnet by Camillo Conti.

[16] Scala, *Teatro delle favole*, 273.

game of mistaken identities, which, through his ignorance, he unwittingly amplifies. Susceptible to magic and superstition, he is easily fooled by Pedrolino, who pretends to be a necromancer and agrees to help him court a pilgrim girl he has fallen in love with. Later, Pedrolino reveals that, to "enjoy" the pilgrim girl, Burattino must remain mute for three days and, if he speaks, he will become a ghost. From this moment on, Burattino is at the center of the scene with a flurry of entrances of lively comicality. In the grip of an insane terror, he does not speak but gesticulates with "hand signs," "nods," "mute acts," and "demonic" behaviors, struggling among the blows of the characters. His madness and terror grow when he is induced to speak, after which he believes he is possessed, and the comedy ends, once again, with his public humiliation: "Burattino: arrives, saying he is bewitched, acts like a possessed man. Pedrolino: says that this is a joke. Burattino: says that, no matter what, he feels like a ghost and is rabid with hunger. Petrolino reveals the truth to him, and here ends the comedy."[17]

Burattino's most emblematic qualities, as developed in Scala's scenarios, return as the main leitmotif in another work, the only one that presents Burattino as the protagonist in its very title, *Le disgratie di Burattino, Commedia ridicolosa e buffonesca* [The Misfortunes of Burattino, Commedia dell'Arte] by Francesco Gattici, first published in 1628.[18]

Gattici's version of Burattino recalls the already popular one of a servant and impish mischief-maker publicly mocked and punished for his foolishness; the same version had appeared in such scenarios as Scala's *Portalettere*.[19] In the *Disgratie*, Burattino is at the center of a complex love triangle, this time between Lavinia and her two suitors, old master Pantalone and young Grisostomo. Burattino attracts a variety of misfortunes by inadvertently entering into delicate relationships and arousing, for lack of caution, the enmity of powerful people with whom he comes

---

[17] Ibid., 281.

[18] In all probability, in addition to being a writer of theatrical texts, Gattici was the author of *Zecca aritmetica*, an intriguing book-game where numbers are used as an instrument for an aristocratic type of entertainment show, not far from the world of street performers. Four comedies by Gattici were published in the 1620s in Rome, Milan, and Venice and then partly reprinted in Milan by Gioseffo Marelli in 1671. Among the comedies chosen for the Milan reprint, one can also find what is now a rare work, *Le disgratie di Burattino*, published for the first time in 1628 by Grignan.

[19] Scala, *Teatro delle favole*, 238.

into contact. By allowing his master's gifts for Lavinia to be stolen and by serving as an intermediary between her and Grisostomo in exchange for free food, he earns the hatred of Pantalone; being, moreover, the servant of the latter, he makes himself hated by Grisostomo. As a secret messenger, he also attracts the resentment of Lavinia's brother, who will eventually use him as a scapegoat to avoid a confrontation with the two suitors. Amid all this turmoil, Burattino continues to act as a servant to multiple masters, his judgment clouded by hunger, but he is finally arrested on the charge of being a thief and is sentenced to prison. Not even Lavinia will come to his rescue, preferring instead to deny ever having had anything to do with him. The intervention of Doctor Graziano will end up worsening the situation by replacing Burattino's imprisonment with a whipping administered in the public square.

Both the Burattino of Gattici and Scala are victims of deception by ill-intentioned agents. At the opening of Gattici's comedy, we witness the arrival of Burattino with a basketful of delicacies and jewels, a gift from Pantalone to his beloved; he ends up in the clutches of two scoundrels who attract him with false flattery and promises of wealth and friendship, alternating between distracting him and emptying his basket.[20] In Scala's *Burle d'Isabella*, Burattino is similarly targeted.

Burattino comes with a basketful of food and says that he wants to eat four mouthfuls before entering the tavern, and he sits down in the middle of the scene to eat. One of them [the two scoundrels] begins to tell Burattino about the country of Cuccagna, and while he is telling him about the opulent life of that country, his companion is eating [from Burattino's basket]. When he has finished eating, he begins to tell him about the punishment given to those who want to work, and in the meantime, the other companion eats too, and between the two of them, they eat everything, and so on. Burattino becomes aware of the trick and, returns home weeping.[21]

Perhaps, at this point, the reader will have remembered another similar hoax, albeit distant in time, also perpetrated against an unfortunate puppet by two shady characters, namely the deception of the Cat and the Fox against Pinocchio in Carlo Collodi's masterpiece.

---

[20] Francesco Gattici, *Le disgratie di Burattino* (Milan: Gioseffo Marelli, 1671), 11–13.
[21] Scala, *Teatro delle favole*, 57.

The association between the two works may seem surprising, still it emerges from several commonalities, including the themes of a task poorly done or shunned, illusions and mirages of easy gratification, and the amplification of misfortune in a series of misadventures. Furthermore, on a textual level, the two works share a preoccupation with wood and fish that goes from histrionic wordplay to fantastic materializations.[22] Pinocchio, who has risen to represent Italian puppet theater throughout the world, largely falls within the contours of Burattino's character and unites, in a suggestive way, the soul of the *zanni* with that of the wooden head.

Burattino, the protagonist of the tradition of Italian piazzas' improvisational theater—who, as we have seen, was marked by persecution, whether through the murder of its interpreter or the disgrace of the character—became emblematic of the growing opposition to the *lazzi* and masks of the commedia dell'arte, which were harshly criticized by religious institutions and the frequent object of bans. The characteristics associated with such theater were then relegated to a more popular expression of Italian theater, tellingly renamed *teatro dei burattini*. The moment in which Mangiafuoco's puppets recognize and enthusiastically embrace Pinocchio, welcoming him as a brother who has returned home after a long absence, now acquires a broader meaning; not only is it a return of Pinocchio to his nature as a puppet, but it is also a return of the ancient mask of Burattino, lost over the centuries, in which the puppets recognize themselves.

We are thus presented with a fascinating panorama of reenactments, where misfortune and marginality have from the very beginning played a central role in the identity of the wooden heads and continued to influence Italian art and culture through different periods and movements. As we will see in this book, the subterranean force of the puppets will give voice to the oppressed and the weak, whether they be laborers on strike

---

[22] Because of its hardness and simplicity, Gattici's character often uses expressions that metaphorically draw on wood to talk about himself. In the prologue, he describes himself in the third person as "a man rough and uncouth as a wooden beam" (*"huomo rozzo, e grosso come un trave"*) and then, answering one of the scoundrels, as being "thick as wood, but subtle as stone" (*"gros de legnam, ma sutil de marmuria"*). See Gattici, *Disgratie di Burattino*, 2, 13. Already in Gattici's work, we find the motif of the puppet-fish, later made famous by the story of Pinocchio, an analogy set in motion by the semantic sphere of the hoax-net metaphor. Thus, when he spots Burattino approaching, the scoundrel Tarantiello declares: "Now, now it's time to throw the net that here is coming a small tench" (*"Mò, mò è lo tiempo da dar la riete allo piesce che n'è isciuta na tenchariella piciarilla"*). See Gattici, *Disgratie di Burattino*, 11.

or children frustrated by the conflicts of the adult world, as shown by works sensitive to the struggle for social justice. Conversely, the puppet's marginality will sometimes represent a superhuman, intimate, and uncontaminated grace; as a source of poetic vitality, it will be the object of rediscovery by writers and moviemakers.

CHAPTER 3

The Remediation of the Puppet: Theater of Animation and Early Cinema

Abstract This chapter questions the common idea that the popular puppet theater disappeared with the arrival of the new medium of cinema. It proposes an assessment of the dynamics of remediation occurring between the older and newer forms of entertainment. The analysis includes cases of intermedial references, both implicit and explicit, revealing how puppetry and early cinema related to and affected one another in a rivalry for spectacle and novelty. The material includes discussions of turn-of-the-century magic lantern slides, puppet show posters, and films such as *Inferno* (1911), *Pinocchio* (1911), and *Cabiria* (1914).

Keywords Puppets · Italian puppetry · Italian cinema · The magic lantern · Remediation · Pinocchio · Puppetry in early cinema · Miniaturization · *Cabiria* · *Inferno* · Narrative frame

In framing the relationship between cinema and puppet theater, it prevails a nostalgic vision, based on the idea of the disappearance of puppets, victims of the success of the new cinematic medium. Words such as those of theater historian Giancarlo Pretini exemplify this point of view: "Cinema developed thanks to traveling artists at the beginning of a journey that changed the taste of the public in just a few years,

F. Pacchioni, *The Image of the Puppet in Italian Theater, Literature and Film*, https://doi.org/10.1007/978-3-030-98668-1_3

supplanting shows that had been rooted in popular culture for centuries, so much so that, to give just one example, puppets and marionettes almost disappeared."[1] The gradual transformation of theaters into cinemas and the progressive economic decline of puppet theater in Italy are incontrovertible facts, though, by the end of the 1900s, puppetry eventually found new spaces adapting to unfolding anthropological and cultural transformations. Rather than speaking of the disappearance of the puppet theater, it would be more correct to speak of the gradual disappearance of its traditional social space during the twentieth century. This change was not only because of the rise of cinema but also because of a series of factors such as the rise of bourgeois realist theater and variety shows, the spread of television, and the move from a family economic model (on which many of the puppet companies were based) to one of individualistic consumerism.

The purely historical perspective that highlights the triumph of cinema in popular entertainment to the detriment of more traditional forms, such as puppets, should be complemented by an aesthetic–cultural perspective able to reveal the relationship of reciprocal influence between the two media. The most significant aspects of this relationship are phenomena of intermediality that are often little known or examined only in a fragmentary way but that nevertheless help clarify the *cultural function* of puppet theater in Italy in broader terms. The ancient traditions of popular theater are employed within the aesthetic fabric of the new medium in the context of pre-cinema and during the first years of the development of the industry, a fact that certainly complicates the commonly shared idea of the disappearance of puppet theater. A more comprehensive analysis of this relationship demonstrates how popular forms of performance, such as puppet theater, were incorporated into new types of entertainment, such as cinema and animated film, and the significance of this development.

The concept of *intermediality* is applied in this book not as a synonym of intertextuality but rather as a research axis that examines the phenomenon of crossing media boundaries within a historical perspective. This relationship is followed in its types of explicit and implicit references, that is, when the medium of cinema refers to puppetry thematically or when it attempts to imitate or evoke expressive conventions related to puppet theater.[2] We will see, however, how the traditional distinction

---

[1] Giancarlo Pretini, *Dalla Fiera al Luna Park* (Udine: Trapezio, 1984), 117.

[2] Other examples of explicit references are the appearance of cinema in a literary work in which the title of a film or the name of a director is mentioned and vice versa. Examples

between implicit and explicit references is not entirely feasible in some cases because, even in apparently more documentary texts, the puppet often performs a profound poetic function, as well as a thematic one, influencing the expressive fabric of the entire work.

After its first explosion in 1897, the cinematograph, still lacking the industrial infrastructure that was established in Europe in the following decade, lived on thanks mainly to the work of itinerant artists. Although closely linked in its evolution to a certain bourgeois and aristocratic scientific and experimental culture, cinema has its roots in the world of barkers, street or fairground entertainers constantly searching for tricks and attractions. Cinema was a "portentous machine of wonders" that combined science and magic and lived in fairs, squares, circuses, and theaters, alternating with moments of musical entertainment, variety shows, mime, and puppet theater shows.[3] For about ten years, cinema developed side by side with the shows of classical puppet theater, with which it shared social contexts and entertainment strategies.[4]

As David Trotter points out in his study on the relationship between modernist literature and cinema at the beginning of the twentieth century, cinema can indeed be considered an art, but it is first and foremost a medium, and as such, it overlaps with other forms of spectacle, in part replicating them.[5] Given the stylistic proximity between theater and cinema, intertwining at the level of staging, the relationship seems to be

---

of implicit references are the *ekphrasis* present in Giorgio Vasari's descriptions, in Klee and Kandinsky's attempts to musicalize painting, and in the recreation of Pontormo's deposition in Pier Paolo Pasolini's film, *Ricotta*. See Werner Wolf, *Intermediality*, in *Routledge Encyclopedia of Narrative Theory*, ed. David Herman, Manfred Jahn, and Marie-Laure Ryan (London, 2005), 252–256; Irina Rajewsky, "Intermediality, Intertextuality, and Remediation: A Literary Perspective on Intermediality," *Intermédialités* 6 (2005): 43–64; Agnes Pethő, "Intermediality in Film: A Historiography of Methodologies," *Film and Media Studies*, 2 (2010): 39–72.

[3] In André Gaudreault's famous division, the first decades of cinema's life are divided into two phases: the cinema of attraction, which expresses cinema primarily as a sensational view (1985–1905), and the cinema of narrative integration, characterized by the development of the conventions of filmic narrative and the relationship between literature and cinema (1905–1915). A. Gaudreault, *Cinema delle origini, o, della "cinematografia-attrazione,"* trans. Viva Paci (Milan: Il Castoro, 2004), 36–49.

[4] Aldo Bernardini, *Cinema italiano delle origini: Gli ambulanti* (Udine: La cineteca del Friuli, 2001), 14–15.

[5] David Trotter, *Cinema and Modernism* (Oxford: Blackwell Publishing, 2007), 3.

immediately complicated by exchanges that go beyond parallelism and imply aesthetic analogies at various levels.

Extending the postmodern idea of the study of culture as a study of media, Fredric Jameson explained how traditional arts should also be considered media and, as such, not necessarily unrelated to concepts and dynamics studied in more modern and contemporary media.[6] The integration that early cinema makes of popular types of attraction, including puppetry, presents the dynamics of competition studied in recent digital contexts, particularly virtual reality and video games, both of which incorporate the experience of previous media (e.g., literature, cinema, theater) in order to surpass it. Therefore, to apply conceptual tools, such as remediation, to the study of the relationship between cinema and puppet theater is not inappropriate. The concept of *remediation*, as theorized by Jay David Bolter and Richard Grusin, according to which "a medium in our culture can never operate in isolation, because it must enter into relationships of respect and rivalry with other media," helps to describe the aesthetic-political nuances of intermedial relationships even in the context of more traditional media.[7] Although the remediation of puppetry in cinema resurfaced from time to time throughout the whole of the twentieth century, it is in the early period when cinema entered the cultural scene negotiating its own place, that one can study fascinating examples of competition and a general readjustment and redefinition among the arts.

The Magic Lamp offers itself as a good starting point in examining the relationship between puppet theater and early cinema. During the eighteenth and nineteenth centuries, puppetry, shadow theater, and the magic lamp travelled throughout Europe. These three forms of spectacle share their ability to be used for popular entertainment, allowing the lower classes to enjoy exotic and awe-inspiring scenes not otherwise accessible. These types of attractions were also used by the educated class for their ability to express a philosophical representation of human life as games or domestic spectacle that the aristocracy could enjoy without having to mix with lower classes. Shadow animation and magic lamps are based on the fascination for the silhouette, the difference being that the magic lamp,

---

[6] Fredric Jameson, *Postmodernism: Or the Cultural Logic of Late Capitalism* (Durham, NC: Duke University Press, 1991), 68.

[7] Jay David Bolter and Richard Grusin, *Remediation: Understanding New Media* (Cambridge, MA: MIT Press, 1999), 65.

using interchangeable slides, allows for more precise control of colors and images. Magic lamp slides were constructed and animated in increasingly sophisticated ways, containing mechanisms operated by levers, knobs, and cords. Animated slides offered a meeting ground between puppet theater and pre-cinema because they often drew on the world of popular street entertainment and, in some cases, contained within them miniature puppets with moving joints.

The important collections housed in the Museo del Precinema e della Lanterna Magica of Padua and the Museo Nazionale del Cinema of Turin make it possible to study the systems of image animation used by lantern makers and, with the many slides of English and French production, open an international horizon to the intermedial dynamics in question. In the performances of the lanternists, slides aiming at pure entertainment—based on mechanisms with levers, masks, or pulls, and reproducing circus and street artists—were probably reserved for the beginning part of the show to entice the audience; but references to previous forms of entertainment such as circus, clowns and puppets were also integrated to be surpassed (note that the mechanical puppet is present inside the slides for magic lanterns in numerous human and animal forms; see Fig. 3.1). These shows tended to progress toward increasingly complex and cinematic visual effects, often culminating in an impressive display of color, abstract shapes, and astronomical visions thanks to the use of overlapping circular glass slides (chromatropes).[8]

Among the materials in the Turin depository are glass slides that explicitly reference English puppetry, including one containing a show of Punch and Judy with interchangeable animated brass figurines and one containing a puppet show with a black figurine (Fig. 3.2). The slide with the Punch and Judy is fascinating because it accurately evokes the theatrical experience associated with this type of British glove puppet show, which has its roots in Neapolitan Pulcinella theater. The performance is shown in the street; it has a barker with drum and flute and a mixed audience in terms of class and age. Offering the animation of various characters, in this case, the slide becomes a tiny theater, radically hybridizing its nature and therefore the experience of projection

[8] See the critical notes of the catalog of the Zotti Minici collection of the museum in Padua and in particular the chapter on animation mechanisms: Carlo Alberto Zotti Minici, *Magiche visioni prima del cinema: La collezione Minici Zotti* (Padova: Il Poligrafo, 2001), 154–156.

Fig. 3.1 Examples of animated slides for magic lantern containing articulated silhouettes. (© Museo del Cinema di Torino)

according to the need to incorporate forms of puppet theater by over-coming them on the level of miniaturization and in the systematic nature of reproduction. Puppets and marionettes become projections of light for the first time, and the play of light projections is in turn intertwined with the audience's contemporary theatrical experiences. These slides show the expressive need of pre-cinema to integrate forms of entertainment familiar

Fig. 3.2 Examples of animated slides for magic lantern containing references to puppet shows (© Museo del Cinema di Torino)

to the audience through explicit reference but also to implicitly incorporate their attractive power through simple miniature automata in the form
of mechanical brass figurines.

On the other hand, puppet theater also tried to confront the dizzying
wonder of animated photography and assimilate the new rivaling medium.
Among the materials collected from the period is the playbill of a performance by the Salvi brothers at Teatro Garibaldi in Padua on April 7, 1900
(Fig. 3.3). In addition to reminding us that puppet theater was not only
a nomadic reality but also an art rooted in urban contexts, this docu-
ment allows us to observe further modalities of the relationship between
theater and cinema in this period. The advertisement of the evening at
the Teatro Garibaldi not only demonstrates a case of coexistence between
puppet theater and early cinema but is also an example of their complex
relationship of aesthetic–economic symbiosis.

The playbill program follows an order of progression in terms of
exceptionality and modernity, starting with the "mechanical puppets" and
concluding with the grand finale of the "animated photographs obtained
with the Lumière cinematograph," passing through various effects and
spectacles of light. The emphasis on the mechanical quality of the show
(whose finale is announced as a "mechanical scenario of great illusion")
is here a pseudoscientific pose typical of the shows of the time aimed at
giving the illusion that the show contained automata.[9] Even more interesting is the way in which traditional rhetorical advertising methods for
puppet shows are altered. Within the progression of the show, cinema
is undoubtedly placed as the event of greatest novelty and visual spectacle. Dramatic value, however, remains the domain of the puppet show
centered on the depiction of *Il povero fornaretto di Venezia* [The Poor
Young Baker of Venice], which promises to strike a wide range of chords:
tragedy, comedy, politics, and redemption. While the puppeteers make use
of the novelty of cinema to attract a larger audience than that of the usual
theater appointment, cinema remains a guest in the "GRAND PALACE"
of puppets.

---

[9] During the nineteenth and early twentieth centuries, European puppeteers and marionette makers resorted to the adjective *mechanical* to attract potential audiences. A case
of spectacle that instead presented automata put into operation by mechanisms and levers
was the German Teatrum Mundi. See John McCormick and Bennie Pratasik, *Popular
Puppet Theater in Europe 1800–1914* (Cambridge: Cambridge University Press, 2004),
66.

PENULTIMA RAPPRESENTAZIONE
TEATRO GARIBALDI
GRANDIOSO EDIFICIO
di MARIONETTE MECCANICHE
e Cinematografo Lumière
dei Fratelli SALVI
Sabato 7 Aprile 1900, alle ore 19.45 (7 3/4 pom.)
Si rappresenta il grandioso spettacolo storico in 5 atti
IL POVERO FORNARETTO DI VENEZIA
ovvero
Il tremendo Consiglio dei Dieci
con ARLECCHINO gondoliere
e FACANAPA custode dei pazzi a S. Servolo
l'ultima parte terminerà colla gloria del Fornaretto nel Paradiso degli innocenti, scenario meccanico di grande illusione.
Parte Seconda
GRANDE NOVITÀ
POLIORAMA MECCANICO
Vedute disolventi, stelle di cromotropo
coi giuochi prismatici e diamantini
Questo nuovo divertimento verrà alternato dalle belle proiezioni di
fotografie animate ottenute col
CINEMATOGRAFO LUMIÉRE
rappresentando le più interessanti novità
SPETTACOLO ECCEZIONALE
Prezzi Serali
Ingresso alla platea, prima galleria ed ai palchi (indistintamente) Cent. 40
Ingresso al loggione (indistintamente) Cent. 25
Poltrone in platea e in prima galleria (oltre l'ingresso) Cent. 50
Scanni in platea e prima galleria Cent. 25
Domani Domenica ultima recita
Addio di FACANAPA
PENULTIMA RAPPRESENTAZIONE

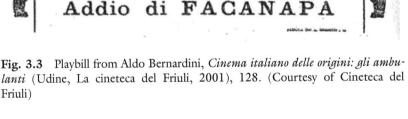

Fig. 3.3 Playbill from Aldo Bernardini, *Cinema italiano delle origini: gli ambulanti* (Udine, La cineteca del Friuli, 2001), 128. (Courtesy of Cineteca del Friuli)

Concluding the puppet show with a film projection is a practice also found in southern Italian puppet theater, as in the cases of the Teatro di Grasso Sicilia and the itinerant theater of Antonino Mancuso.[10] Puppet theater and cinema shared a single evening or space in these settings, in theaters as well as outdoor arenas, sometimes transforming the former into multifunctional venues, with a screen for projection on one side and the stage on the other (as was also the case with the northern Braga family in Udine). The inability or impossibility of achieving integration evidently led to conflictual situations such as that of San Giuseppe Iato, where Gaspare Canino's theater was forced to close and move to another town because of pressure from a local cinema.[11]

On the other side of the arena, silent cinema demonstrates the need to refer to puppet theater by integrating its dramatic value and stage effects. The marionette was used as a special effect in *Inferno* (1911), a film that marked a step forward in the process of legitimizing cinema in Italy by placing itself in a dignified position in adapting both Dante's epic poem and Gustave Doré's illustrations. Among the rich and pioneering special effects of *Inferno* is a puppet of the monster Cerberus, whose three heads are operated by wires (Fig. 3.4), as well as the use of forced perspective, as for example in the encounter with Pluto.

In the same year, *Pinocchio*, directed by Giulio Antamoro and produced by the Roman Cines, was released. Among the most interesting scenes of the film is the arrival at Mangiafuoco's theater: Pinocchio, having sneaked in through the back without paying, finds himself in a warehouse filled with puppets, which, despite being played by live actors, are striking for the rigidity with which they fall. After welcoming Pinocchio, the puppets begin the show. At this point, the frame is divided into two parts to allow for double exposure and false perspective: at the bottom on the right, the cheering audience, and, in the corner on the left, live actors effectively playing puppets and moving like them. The double exposure allows for the illusion of height difference between the puppets and Mangiafuoco when he calls them before him (Fig. 3.5). Important to note is the gestural expressiveness of Ferdinand Guillaume (alias Polidor or Tontolini, 1887–1977) in the role of Pinocchio because the acting in

[10] See Marcella Croce, *Pupi carretti contastorie* (Palermo, Dario Flaccovio Editore: 1999), 14.

[11] John McCormick, Alfonso Cipolla, and Alessandro Napoli, *The Italian Puppet Theater: A History* (Jefferson, NC: McFarland & Company, 2010), 80–81.

Fig. 3.4 Screenshot from *L'inferno* (dir. Giuseppe de Liguoro, Francesco Bertolini, Adolfo Padova, 1911), DVD

Fig. 3.5 Screenshot from *Pinocchio* (dir. Giulio Antamoro, Cines, 1911), DVD

this film can be considered one of the first cinematic manifestations of puppet imitation, a style that would become very successful during the twentieth century, as we will see in the example of Totò; not coincidentally, Federico Fellini would later celebrate Polidor by inserting him as a melancholic clown in *La dolce vita* (1960).

The year 1914 marks the beginning of the great national and international parable of Vittorio Podrecca's (1883–1959) marionette company, as well as the release of *Cabiria*, a film that impacted the history of Italian and world cinema. In this film, puppet theatricality is perceived as much in macroscopic influences as in microscopic references. As historian Alfonso Cipolla rightly notes, Giovanni Pastrone's (1883–1959) film "draws, above all, from the marionette theater, in terms of melodrama, subjects, genres, and spectacularism"; therefore, "the constitutive elements that determine the [film's] genre, such as the exotic-pagan setting, the violence of nature, the sacrifice, the collapse of the temple can be all traced precisely ... to much of the puppet repertoire of the time."[12]

Moreover, in the first frames of the film is a careful reference to an ancient game, the same game that probably developed over the centuries into the form of street theater known today as *planchette* or *marionette a tavoletta* (plank marionette). Against the backdrop of a Roman villa, the nurse Croessa is teaching little Cabiria the workings of two puppets moved by a rope running through them (Fig. 3.6), an image that closely mirrors the illustration of the *ludus monstrorum* (amazing game) contained in the twelfth-century Latin treatise *Hortus deliciarum*.[13] Just as in the ancient game, the film scene shows the puppets moved by hands, whereas in *marionette a tavoletta*, the rope is tied to the leg of the puppeteer, who can then play a musical instrument with his hands and simultaneously stage a hilarious dance in the street (a trick typically used by bagpipers and ocarinists).[14]

The choice to use this particular type of puppet in *Cabiria* is therefore based on an erudite hypothesis of the existence of this game in Roman

---

[12] A. Cipolla, *L'Italia*, in *Il mondo delle figure. Burattini, marionette, pupi, ombre*, ed. Luigi Allegri and Manuela Bambozzi (Rome: Carocci Editore, 2012), 213.

[13] Ibid., 185.

[14] Anton Giulio Bragaglia, *Pulcinella* (Rome: G. Casini, 1953), 401.

Fig. 3.6   Screenshot from *Cabiria* (dir. Giuseppe Pastrone, Itala Film Torino, 1914), DVD

times, but it is arguably more important to examine the symbolic function that the game plays in the film. In fact, the two puppets that appear in the opening scene allude to a Roman soldier and a girl, an image that suggests the turbulent fate of the young Cabiria and her rescuer, Fulvio Axilla, bound the capricious jolts of a string, coming closer and then moving apart. This dynamic is at the heart of the film's plot, in which, according to the critic Paolo Cherchi Usai, "everything... happens out of the revenge or the goodwill of fate."[15]

The latter is a minimal and circumscribed case of intermediality, yet this cinematic strategy incorporates the potential for immediacy and the fascination with miniaturization, both of which are the strengths of the puppet theater. A similar meta-narrative move, hidden in an apparently casual reference to the puppet show, will later be found applied in a more elaborate way in a film such as *I bambini ci guardano* (*The Children Are Watching Us*, Vittorio De Sica, 1944), where an opening scene with a violent Puncinella show foreshadows the film's family dynamics. Also,

---

[15] Paolo Cherchi Usai, *Giovanni Pastrone. Gli anni d'oro del cinema di Torino* (Turin: Strenna UTET, 1986), 16.

in the more famous case of *Paisà* (Roberto Rossellini, 1946), where a fight between Christian knights and Saracens in a *pupi* theater reflects the theme of racial conflict.

The relationship between early cinema and puppet theater is not reduced to a simple replacement of the latter but rather is a dialogic and complex process of remediation; moreover, this intermedial relationship confirms the permanent aesthetic–cultural vitality of the puppet theater across media and national borders. Starting with the animated slides for magic lanterns, which integrate, even in radical ways, the reference to puppetry, and moving through sporadic cases of films such as *Pinocchio*, *L'Inferno*, and *Cabiria*, we can observe a progressive appropriation of the tradition of popular theater and the qualities of the puppet. The magic of the animated object is transformed into a spectacle of light that accentuates its special stylized qualities and highlights its narrative framing functions. In this intermedial panorama, puppet theater does not vanish under the advance of cinema but rather continues to live within the body of the new and triumphant cinematographic medium to then reach, as this book intends to show, moments of great sophistication and depth.

CHAPTER 4

The Uncanny Marionette: Avant-Garde and Intermedial Experimentation

Abstract In this chapter, the author accounts for the marionette's capacity to imitate and miniaturize the human body in movement and finds in this trait the root of the marionette's extraordinary success in Europe. Additionally, the marionette's realism is connected to the psycho-analytic notion of the uncanny, which allows for psychological depth in films featuring the collaboration of Italian puppeteers, such as *I'm Suzanne* (1933). At the same time, the uncanny limits the relationship between puppets and film, as shown in various digital animation and puppet films, such as the unique case of *I quattro moschettieri* (1936), and it plays an internationally central role in the horror and sci-fi genres, as well as in experimental filmmaking.

Keywords Puppets · Italian puppetry · Italian American · Hollywood · The uncanny · Vittorio Podrecca · Puppets in film and television · Remediation · Collaboration · Miniaturization · Horror · Experimental filmmaking · Jan Švankmajer · Carlo Campogalliani

The Italian marionette theater became popular during the second half of the eighteenth century and reached its peak in the nineteenth century, especially in the large cities of the center and north of Italy, such as Milan, Turin, Venice, Genoa, and Rome. Turin is often cited as an example

© The Author(s), under exclusive license to Springer Nature Switzerland AG 2022
F. Pacchioni, *The Image of the Puppet in Italian Theater, Literature and Film*, https://doi.org/10.1007/978-3-030-98668-1_4

thanks to the availability of documentation demonstrating the increase in the number of performances staged in the city, which multiplied from forty to three hundred in the second half of the eighteenth century. During the nineteenth century, the stable northern companies, led by the Lupi and Colla families and by artists of outstanding talent such as Giuseppe Fiando, Antonio Reccardini, and Rinaldo and Luciano Zane, were able to develop a vast repertoire. Scholar Alfonso Cipolla reminds us that the marionette theater was "conceived based on the magnificence of the productions, which were not only able to emulate but also able to compete with the productions of the great opera houses, both types of shows being based on the richness of the scenery, especially as far as dance scenes were concerned."[1]

Toward the end of the nineteenth century, the modern marionette, increasingly complex in its articulations, strongly expressed the illusion and miniaturization of the human body in motion. The development of the naturalistic qualities of the marionette received a considerable boost from the arrival of Thomas Holden's English marionette in 1885. Unlike the Italian models, which still had a fixed central control bar, Holden's marionettes were moved entirely by wires, which allowed for more complex articulations. Italian artists soon adapted to the new type of marionette, and this naturalistic research found its apex in the activity of Vittorio Podrecca (1883–1959), starting in 1914 when he opened his Teatro dei Piccoli.[2] Podrecca's company, then one of the best-known Italian theatrical troupes internationally, was a formative experience for other pioneers of puppetry such as Maria Signorelli (1908–1992); at the same time, it influenced different artistic domains, including the work of the futurist Fortunato Depero (1892–1960), who drew from Podrecca's techniques and ideas for his well-known *Balli Plastici* [Plastic Dances] (1917).[3]

[1] A. Cipolla, *L'Italia*, cit., 205.

[2] Ibid., pp. 208–209. For a more in-depth study on both Holden's and Podrecca's influence, see Alfonso Cipolla and Giovanni Moretti, *Commedianti figurati e attori pupazzani: Testimonianze di moralisti e memorialisti, viaggiatori e cronisti per una storia del teatro con le marionette e con i burattini in Italia* (Turin: Linea Teatrale, 2003), 169–181.

[3] Of course, the rapport between low and high brow culture should not come as surprise. As Scott Cutler Shershow has amply demonstrated in his *Puppets & "Popular" Culture* (Ithaca: Cornel UP, 1995)—a study that also focuses on puppet as cultural

In 1933 we find the Podrecca company shoulder to shoulder with the American Yale Puppeteers for *I Am Suzanne!* directed by Rowland Lee. In this film, which employs the artifice of miniaturization, Italian artistry not only creates the stage effects but also functions as a central theme.[4] *I Am Suzanne!* stages a tormented love story between an Italian American puppeteer, Tony Malatini (played by Gene Raymond), and the dancer Suzanne (played by Lilian Harvey). After an accident, Suzanne must retire from the stage for a time and undergoes an identity crisis accentuated by her growing involvement with the puppeteer and the world of his theater. Marionettes are used to weave the deep psychological plot of the film, which is linked to the dimension of Suzanne's nightmares. This happens, for example, in the sequence in which the dancer is put on trial by the marionettes and in which the human characters of the film are called as witnesses to the accusation. In the nightmare, their human nature is mixed up with that of the inanimate puppets, as their legs dangle in the void and the actors' words become repetitive. These facts generate the anguish expressed by Suzanne's face shot in close-up, making explicit the feeling of the uncanny (Fig. 4.1).

The concept of the uncanny, which in Italian can be expressed by the term *perturbante*, was devised to describe the sensation that one feels in front of an ontologically ambiguous object that lies between the inanimate and the animate, just as in the case of puppets and verisimilar automata. It is important to remember that since the first studies of this phenomenon—that is, the essay of 1906 by Ernst Jentsch followed by the more famous essay by Sigmund Freud in 1919—the sensation of the

---

representation, but primarily in early modern and modern England—the cases of inter-penetration between high and low cultures are many and the two cannot be rigidly separated.

[4] A very different collaboration involved the company of the eclectic Yambo, the stage name of Enrico Novelli (1874–1943), and the director Carmine Gallone (1885–1973) for the 1939 film *Marionette*. This is a romance film centered on the figure of the opera singer Beniamino Gigli (1890–1957), which nonetheless includes valuable and accurate theatrical shots, such as those of a crowded and grandiose marionette theater staging of the musical opera *Fra Diavolo*, during which the singer lends his voice to the bandit for the famous aria. In this film, puppetry remains part of the background, except for a veiled hint at the theme of doubles present in an interesting sequence where a marionette show reveals the love dynamics between the film's characters. In the title, but also in its emphasis on the invisible threads of the passions that control the characters, Gallone's film refers to the grotesque comedy by Pier Maria Rosso di San Secondo (1887–1956), *Marionette, Che Passione!* (published by Treves in 1926 but written in 1918).

Fig. 4.1   Screenshots from *I am Susanne!* (dir. Rowland V. Lee, 1933), DVD

uncanny has not been limited to direct encounters with the object but is also analyzed in the literary field, as for example in the emblematic story *The Sandman*, by E. T. A. Hoffman, which attests to the beginning of the relevance of this concept in the artistic field.[5] *I am Suzanne!* contains numerous scenes that express the uncanny effect in more or less explicit ways, among which the film's finale stands out for its spectacular infernal dance where human bodies alternate with marionettes and where Suzanne is transformed from an objectified victim, and therefore a puppet, into a triumphant figure who emerges in all her physical glory, having finally regained her ability as a dancer.

Besides illustrating the relevance of the intermedial (and intercultural) encounter between the Podrecca company's Italian marionette theater and American cinema, the case of *I Am Suzanne!* expresses the vital link between modern puppetry and the uncanny, specifically around the notion of the uncanny valley.[6] As is well known, the latter relationship, which has reached its most acute and strident levels in the horror genre,

---

[5] Ernest Jentsch, "On the Psychology of the Uncanny," *Angelaki* 2, no. I, (1997): 7–16; first published in *Psychiatrisch-Neurologische Wochenschrift* 8.22, 25 (August, 1906): 195–198 and 8.23 (1 September 1906): 203–205; Sigmund Freud, *Il perturbante* (Napoli: Theoria, 1998); first edition: "The Uncanny," *Imago* 5–6 (1919): 297–324; Ernst Theodor Amadeus Hoffmann, "The Sandman," in *The Tales of Hoffmann* (New York: Frederick Ungar Publisher, 1963), 1–34; first edition: "The Sandman," in *Die Nachtstücke*, first printing (Berlin: Reimer, 1817).

[6] The concept, first used in robotics to measure the level of perceived naturalness of human simulacra, points to an area of humanoid likeness where the simulacrum, too close to a real human figure yet clearly still non-human, causes cognitive confusion and anxiety.

explores the primitive roots of the phenomenon by playing at times with alchemical myths—see the extended series of *The Puppet Master* (1989–2020) with its varied cast of lethal puppets—and at other times with the transmigration of the spirit, exemplified by the successful series *Child's Play* (1988–2020) with its terrifying serial-killer doll Chucky. In Italy, the pioneers of horror are certainly not alien to the expressive potential of the uncanny in relation to the puppet, as evidenced by the numerous cases of mechanical puppets and dolls in the hands of special effects geniuses such as Mario Bava (1914–1980), Carlo Rambaldi (1925–2012), and Dario Argento (1940–).

It is not easy to sum up the widespread use of puppetry in cinema without inadvertently slipping into the domains of horror, avant-garde film, or children's entertainment. Jim Henson and his still-active company represent a striking case of success, undoubtedly due to the invention of the *Muppet*, which combines the grace and practicality of the stick puppet with the expressive plasticity of the glove puppet, ideal for shooting television and film—think especially of films directed at young and adult audiences alike such as *The Dark Crystal* (1982) and the remarkable episodic prequel produced by Netflix, *The Dark Crystal: Age of Resistance* (2019).[7] However, an attempt bring into cinema the spectacle of puppetry in its entirety, with its magnificence, dramatic complexity, and ability to entertain a mixed audience, was made in Italy in the unique and rather unknown case of Carlo Campogalliani's (1885–1974) *I quattro moschettieri* [The Four Musketeers] (1936), the only Italian feature film, to my knowledge, cast entirely with marionettes.[8] Because of the unique position it occupies, this film offers itself as an instructive case of the intermedial dynamics between puppet theater and cinema as well as between tradition and modernity in a broader sense.

See: Masahiro Mori, "The Uncanny Valley," *IEEE Robotics and Automation Magazine* (June 2012): 99–100.

[7] In connection to different genres and technologies, see also the case of surreal satire ranging from silhouette animation to puppet films such as *Team America: World Police* (2004), referenced in note 84, as well as the powerful use of puppetry in realizing alien forms in Rockne S. O'Bannon's sci-fi television series *Farscape* (1999–2003).

[8] There exists a short and older film, by an unknown director, containing a brief introductory marionette scene, entitled *Il Risveglio delle Marionette* [The Awakening of the Puppets] from 1914, but it is nothing comparable to Campogalliani's film.

I quattro moschettieri transposes narrative conventions belonging to the marionette theater onto the cinematic plane. The simplicity of the plot is instrumental to the integration of a series of action scenes (chases, fights, and acrobatics), moments of comedy, satirical touches, and scenic effects that evoke the marvelous and the fabulous. As is typical of marionette shows, where even the most dramatic repertoire must be interspersed with moments of pure entertainment, the plot of the film follows the vicissitudes of the famous musketeers as they grapple with an evil sorcerer and his army—accompanied, however, by a hilarious pair of marionettes personifying Laurel and Hardy (Image 12). The choice of inserting the marionettes of the two great comedians into the roles of sidekicks, typically reserved for popular theater duos such as Brighella and Arlecchino or Sandrone and Fagiolino, represents an interesting strategy on Campogalliani's part, a way to merge theater and cinema further, to make the cinema audience feel more comfortable, and to camouflage the marionette in the figure of the actor.

The film's editing is surprisingly familiar, with smooth transitions from establishing shots to double shots and even close-ups (despite the frozen expressions of the puppets). *I quattro moschettieri* conveys high expressive potential—something that will find more and more space in the animated film—the ability to create the entire world of the story in the film and to design the evocative qualities of the mise en scène down to the smallest detail and to a level not easily achieved in a live-action film. Another interesting aspect of this film is found in the action scenes, which are particularly simple compared to their complexity in live-action films. This simplicity is not historically determined or due to the use of rudimentary means; rather, it expresses the lightness that characterizes the marionettes: in their plunges from the castle tower, the figures of the musketeers communicate emancipation from the force of gravity, a superhuman grace of romantic memory.

From the very beginning, *I quattro moschettieri* promises to demonstrate the survival capacity of the puppet show, now inserted in its integrity, power, and traditional coherence into the context of the cinematographic medium. It is not by chance that the film is introduced by a mockumentary preamble, where we see some puppeteers at work and a group of children around a toy theater. At the same time, an emotional voice explains how (even though there are still artists who know how to animate their puppets) puppetry is an ancient game in danger of extinction, inexorably being replaced by modern toys and new means of entertainment.

Just as new forms of media typically advertise themselves by leveraging greater expressive power and realism, older media predictably try to protect their space by accusing new media of immorality; thus, the narrator who introduces *I quattro moschettieri* does not fail to warn that modern media are less "chaste and moral" than traditional ones. It should be noted here that Carlo Campogalliani comes from an Emilian family that was one of the historical cornerstones of Italian puppetry.[9] For a showman such as Campogalliani, to fall back on this moral critique reveals how his film project, while achieving a fine result, was already at that time based on the assumption of historical defeat and a desperate attempt to seek new territories for classical puppet theater in contemporary world.

It is no coincidence that the film contains a series of moments that satirize the technological world: when Laurel and Hardy mistake a donkey for a radio (Fig. 4.2), when the telephone does not work at the very moment when help must be called for, when technology serves as the natural domain of the villains. The film's anti-technological mockery is a sign of the tension inherent in the aesthetic politics of remediation to which the film bears clear and precious witness.

As an example of the challenge that characterizes Italian culture, always called upon to find bridges connecting its traditions to the unstable and often unknown horizons of modernity, the puppet film could have availed itself in Italy of technical knowledge that was highly competitive with other countries. Campogalliani's film did not, however, introduce a new popular genre, and this fertile and singular intersection perhaps remained a missed opportunity. Thanks to the resources of the Italian puppet theater, puppet films could have offered a language capable of giving life to complex and ambitious, yet still popular, works. Perhaps it could have remained a minor Italian expression alongside the Disney animated film, which was beginning its conquest in those very years (*Snow White* arrived in Italy in 1938).[10]

---

[9] For information on Carlo Campogalliani, see Roberto Chiti, José Pantieri, and Paolo Popeschich, *Almanacco del Cinema Muto Italiano* (Forlì: Centro Studi Cinetelevisivi, 1988), 74.

[10] Italian expressions of the puppet movie remained limited to children's television networks, even if with notable success, as in the striking case of Topo Gigio (Gigio the Mouse), which, from the 1960s until the end of the 1980s, was exported to South

Fig. 4.2 Screenshots from *I quattro moschettieri* (dir. Carlo Campogalliani, 1936), digitalized copy kindly provided by the Cineteca of Bologna

Behind these changes were a multitude of factors—including the perception of puppetry as something antiquated (which was accentuated by the capitalist cultural policies of the postwar period)—and certainly also the effect of the uncanny that controls, and in some ways limits, the relationship between puppetry and cinema. The uncanny effect remains an element to be treated with caution in film productions that employ puppets, as well as in digital animation (as the problematic cases of photorealistic films such as Robert Zemeckis's *The Polar Express* and Steven Spielberg's *The Adventures of Tin Tin* teach us), because it can risk making the viewing unpleasant if not disturbing. The effect of the uncanny is considered one of the impediments that has hindered the development of a genre of puppet films beyond the sphere of the deliberately experimental film, in which the Czech Jiří Trinka (1912–1969), Jiří Barta (1948–), and Jan Švankmajer (1934–) excel.

American and European countries and even to Japan. Particularly interesting, precisely because of its roots in the world of puppetry, is *L'Albero Azzurro* (The Blue Tree), broadcast on RAI from the 1990s to the present day.

Even today, as in the past, the puppet film has remained a genre largely alien to the public's tastes, and not only in Italy. Moving on to the first years of the new millennium, the decision to produce a film entirely for puppets continues to be a highly experimental choice, as is clearly demonstrated by *Strings*, released in 2004 and directed by the original Danish director Anders Rønnow Klarlund. This film is an adventure with an epic scope: a young prince comes to uncover, after a long journey, the plot that has led his people to believe that a group of peaceful natives are enemies to be persecuted. The film, made with the help of numerous puppet masters from various parts of Europe, finds in the marionette an ideal instrument to express a spiritual conception of the world, where the strings that mysteriously lose themselves in the sky (like those of the marionette Bululù in Bontempelli's novel analyzed in the following chapter) help explain the cosmic bond that unites all beings, including the two conflicting peoples in the film's story. *Strings* clearly alludes to, and reinterprets through a new-age lens, concepts that once attracted philosophers, writers, and theater practitioners to puppetry, from the romantic realm that extended from Heinrich von Kleist (1777–1811) to Edward Gordon Craig (1872–1966), to the metaphysical expanse that stretched from Bontempelli to Pasolini. This is a guiding thread that leads to a fuller appreciation of the spiritual and ecological value that the metaphor of the marionette expresses, even if indirectly, in films such as James Cameron's *Avatar* (2009). The protagonists in this last case virtually animate extraterrestrial bodies to save an alien indigenous culture capable of living, unlike the terrestrial one, in harmony with the network of natural relationships.

CHAPTER 5

Yearning for Vitality: The Italian Avant-Garde and the Puppet

Abstract This chapter discusses how the puppet image, including its incarnations as mannequin and robot, are employed by the early twentieth-century Italian avant-garde, particularly by futurist and metaphysical artists. Among the works analyzed are Marinetti's *Fantocci elettrici* (1909), Giorgio de Chirico's paintings, Bontempelli's *Siepe a nordovest* (1918) and *Eva ultima* (1922). The puppet image is revealed to relate to the idea of a quest for freedom and vitality, which acquires different forms in relation to the artist's ideological position.

Keywords Puppets · Italian puppetry · Italian theater · Italian literature · Italian painting · Filippo Tommaso Marinetti · Massimo Bontempelli · Giorgio de Chirico · Mannequin · Robot · Automaton · Romance · Futurism · Avant-garde · Metaphysics · Artificial intelligence · Fascism · Remediation

The Italian avant-garde of the early twentieth century had a fascination with the human simulacrum that was pervaded by a mixture of curiosity and bitterness. The mannequin and the marionette were associated with a pining for a greater degree of freedom and vitality and an ideal of humanity that artists understood in different and often antithetical ways. Even when they were close to the world of puppetry, the futurists were

F. Pacchioni, *The Image of the Puppet in Italian Theater, Literature and Film*, https://doi.org/10.1007/978-3-030-98668-1_5

mainly interested in the mechanical evocations of the marionette, as in the aforementioned case of Fortunato Depero's drawing from the technical knowledge of Podrecca's Teatro dei Piccoli within the context of *Balli Plastici*, or in the fascination of artists such as Luciano Folgore (pseudonym of Omero Vecchi, 1888–1966) with the mechanical body of Pinocchio.[1] In the vast sphere of futurism's relationship with technology, the marionette stands as the predecessor of the robot.

Let us take Filippo Tommaso Marinetti's *Fantocci elettrici* [Electric Puppets] as an example. There are different versions of this text in French and Italian, written between 1909 and 1926.[2] In the Italian version, an engineer, Riccardo Marinetti, builds two automata of the opposite sex and places them in his living room to enliven his erotic life through an irreverent and transgressive game that involves his wife. First, the automata allow the engineer to ridicule and override what he calls "the precise framework of life's idiosyncrasies," in other words, established morality; hence the names with which he baptizes them: "Professor Marriage" and "Mrs. Family." Second, the automata, especially when distracted or dormant, enhance the erotic charge of the engineer's furtive courtship with his wife, where eroticism stands for the freedom of imagination and renewal of perceptual faculties.

RICCARDO: Here are the symbols of everything that exists outside of our love, here are the symbols of all the horrible reality: duty, money, virtue, old age, monotony, the boredom of the heart, weariness of the flesh, stupidity of the blood, social laws... and who knows what else!

MARIA: For me, I'd rather kick all those ugly characters out!

RICCARDO: Impossible since they are in us!... Instead, we must play tricks on them, forcing them to act in our way. Right behind their backs, and almost under their noses, we must enjoy all that love has to offer, with its fever of adventure and the unknown, with its scent of rebellion,

---

[1] Folgore's case has been analyzed in Katia Pizzi, "Pinocchio and the Mechanical Body: Luciano Folgore's Papers at the Getty Research Institute Library," in *Pinocchio, Puppets and Modernity*, ed. Katia Pizzi (New York and London: Routledge, 2012), 135–162. On the relationship between puppet theater and futurism in Depero, see A. Cipolla and G. Moretti, *Commedianti figurati e attori pupazzani*, op. cit., 182–184.

[2] Filippo Tommaso Marinetti, *Fantocci elettrici. Sintesi drammatica, Teatro*, IV, 1, 1926, 14–18.

of danger or the impossible, with its violence and its quick manners of a thief caught in the act... I simply want to have close to me, when I kiss you, precise pictures of the laziness of life in order to fly through dreams with you.[3]

Despite the engineer's passionate explanations, his wife refuses to play along and cannot accept the presence of the automata, which make her feel uncomfortable. At her insistence, the engineer decides to throw the electric puppets off the balcony overlooking the sea, and some fishermen immediately mistake them for actual corpses. Strangely enough, the fishermen do not recognize the fiction of the mechanical puppet, not even when the robots are fished out and brought back to the engineer's house. Therefore, the engineer's liberating symbolic game is not appreciated by women or common folk, indicating the sexist and elitist character of Marinetti's revolutionary vision.

Even if the objective of Marinetti's text is to laugh at conventions considered as miserable and oppressive, his automata are bitter emblems of a humanity that is subject to rigid limits and made ridiculous in its predictability. Even for artists such as Giorgio de Chirico and Massimo Bontempelli, encounters with man-made objects aroused an impulse toward the search for vitality. However, de Chirico, closer to classical and traditional culture, preferred statues, mannequins, or puppets to automata. Like De Chirico, Massimo Bontempelli was a master of interweaving the human plane with that of the simulacrum.

In 1918, Bontempelli wrote the musical drama *Siepe a nordovest* [Northwestern Edge], performed in Rome in 1923 at the Teatro degli Indipendenti of Anton Giulio Bragaglia (1890–1960), and published the following year for *Valori Plastici* with illustrations by Giorgio de Chirico. The drama takes place in two dimensions on opposite sides of the stage, the world of the humans and the world of the puppets, separated by a hedge from which a wind blows that evokes a restless sense of the unknown. The vicissitudes of men and puppets, mutually invisible, intertwine for various irrational motives of a political and amorous nature. For both groups, these events are devoid of causal logic and are charged with mystery, which allows the author to unravel the metaphysical discourse at the heart of the drama: man's unawareness of the occult forces that

[3] Ibid., 17–18.

Fig. 5.1 Illustrations by G. de Chirico, from Massimo Bontempelli and Giorgio de Chirico, *Siepe a Nordovest: rappresentazione, prosa e musica di Massimo Bontempelli* (Roma: Edizioni Valori Plastici, 1924)

maneuver him and to which he cannot help but ascribe supernatural values (Fig. 5.1).

At the beginning of the play, this existential circumstance is symbolically expressed by the hammock in which we find one of the main characters, suspended by a thread, in his sleep (Fig. 5.1). Like the humans, the unsuspecting puppets also infer the presence of divine or demonic creatures. Among the characters played by live actors, only two can perceive the invisible reality: the gypsy and, coincidentally, the puppeteer, the former because of his marginalized perspective, detached from the illusions that envelop everyday life, the latter because of his ability to navigate fiction, thanks to his familiarity with the puppet theater. Beneath Bontempelli's drama, there is a desire for freedom that unites men and puppets, a desire for both to emancipate themselves from the unknown forces that maneuver life, to know the world and their place within it fully.

As a result, in *Siepe a nordvest*, we find the insertion of comic-satirical moments is realized through another form of traditional popular theater, *burattini* (glove puppets), which takes place at the side of the stage and on the front side of the curtain. This frame of popular theatricality and playfulness, containing a courtship scene between Napoleon and Columbine, seems to place itself in an intermediate dimension between spectacle and audience. Furthermore, it is precisely the comic and ironic perspective that Bontempelli appears to suggest as a strategy to see beyond, a view that finds its natural expression in the parodic power of the glove puppets, with their disproportionate bodies and lack of legs.

However, in this play, the glove puppets evoke a greater sense of humanity than the flesh-and-blood actors, primarily because of their satirical detachment from their assigned characters or masks, particularly in the case of the Napoleon puppet, whose mockery effectively lowers and desecrates the historical figure.

The collaboration with Giorgio de Chirico helps understand the puppet's meaning in Bontempelli's work. The critic Giorgio Castelfranco thus described the illustrations that de Chirico created for *Siepe a nordvest*:

> This coexistence without communication of men and puppets had a particular flavor of *metaphysical surprise* because the scenic events appeared beyond any logical causality. The scene itself, a slope of hills and gardens, and an uphill staircase leading to a villa beyond the trees was made up of natural elements that de Chirico was observing with new enthusiasm in Rome; above all, the large, old, and thriving trees...[4]

The surreal sensibility that confuses man and object, at the heart of Bontempelli's aesthetics, is wholly in tune with the work of de Chirico, whose paintings made between 1915 and 1918, dominated by the man-statue figure in relation to both window mannequin and theatricality, should be remembered: *Il vaticinatore* (*The Vaticinator*, 1915), *Manichini e torre rosa* (*Mannequins and Pink Tower*, 1915), *Le muse inquietanti* (*The Disquieting Muses*, 1916–18) and *Ettore e Andromaca* (*Hector and Andromache*, 1917).[5] It is de Chirico himself who explains the function of the mannequin in some of his reflections: "the mannequin is profoundly non-living and this lack of life repels us and makes us hate it"; it is an object that should give rise in man to "a frenzied desire to perform great actions, to prove to others and to himself what he is capable of and to demonstrate clearly and once and for all that the mannequin is a slander of man and that we are not, after all, such an insignificant thing that any object can resemble us."[6]

[4] Maurizio Fagiolo dell'Arco, *L'opera completa di de Chirico* (Milano: Rizzoli Editore, 1984), 110.

[5] See Sara Schumacher, "'Man-statue-object' Giorgio de Chirico's Mythologized Mannequin Paintings in Late 1920s Paris" (unpublished doctoral dissertation, University of Oregon, 2007), 27–32.

[6] M. Fagiolo dell'Arco, op. cit., 94. See also Giorgio de Chirico, "Commedia dell'arte moderna," *L'Illustrazione italiana* 35 (1940): 189–197.

Bontempelli further develops the metaphor of the puppet in the novel *Eva ultima* [The Last Eve], published in 1922, set in an unspecified space and time where antiquity and modernity coexist and where people no longer seem to believe in magic, which is nevertheless expressed even in the banalest aspects of everyday life. This novel heralds and exemplifies the perspective of magical realism that Bontempelli later formulated in his magazine *900* while continuing to renew the tradition of the European novel through a parody of futurist techniques and what has been called a "counterfeit of the psychological novel with an erotic-sentimental background."[7]

Bontempelli was directly inspired by *Ève future* [Eve of the Future], a novel published in 1886 by Villiers de l'Isle-Adam (1838–1889), which tells of a man who, after being rejected by a beautiful but insensitive woman, realizes his dreams of love in an encounter with an automaton of beauty and mental refinement greater than those of the beloved woman.[8] However, the protagonist of Bontempelli's novel is an emblematic female character, Eva, who is chosen as "queen" by an equally symbolic male deuteragonist, Evandro, who defines himself as "neither an ordinary man nor a romantic magician."[9] Confused in Evandro's crepuscular realm, Eva cannot help but notice an insurmountable incomprehension between the two of them, as she represents perceptive emotionality, and he represents unflagging rationality.[10]

When Eva asks Evandro for something she can love,[11] he provides her with Bululù, a phantasmagorical and miraculous puppet of profound humility and sensitivity, whose strings rise into the sky, allowing him to move freely through space. In the words of the fortune-teller at the beginning of the novel, Bululù is prophesied as a "new thing... new, impossible and true," with reference to the threads ("your heart forever entangles itself in the net of four threads").[12] Similar to *Ève future*,

[7] Roselena Glielmo, *La traversata dell'ironia* (Salerno: Alfredo Guida Editore, 1994), 78.

[8] Auguste de Villiers de l'Isle-Adam, *L'Ève future* (Parigi: M. de Brunhoff, 1886).

[9] Massimo Bontempelli, *Eva ultima* (Rome: Lucarini, 1988), 115. First edition: *Eva ultima* (Alberto Stock, Rome, 1923).

[10] Ibid., 59, 100–101.

[11] Ibid., 103–110.

[12] Ibid., 24–25.

where the automaton functions as part of an apocalyptic perspective in which humanity has forgotten how to love and is proving inferior to the machine, the puppet in *Eva ultima*, Bululù, highlights the limits of modern man's sensibilities. In Bontempelli, the robot is, however, replaced by a marionette, and the gender of the protagonist is inverted, calling for a return to traditional aesthetics and the senses via feminine intuition. Thus, we are one step beyond the existential parallel between human and puppet expressed in *Siepe a nordvest*. Here, the puppet Bululù, fully aware of his nature, represents the ultimate ideal of authenticity and humanity and is, therefore, the only being that Eva can truly love. Eva is immediately fascinated and disturbed by Bululù and cannot bear to have his puppet nature hinted at or made a spectacle of.[13] Even a bitterly comic character, the Philosopher, emphasizes Bululu's spiritual authenticity, blurring the line between human and non-human with a deduction: "A puppet is a fake man. So, a fake puppet is a fake fake-man, that is, a real man, the real man, the only real man, the real man par excellence!".[14]

Bululù represents the utopia of the Other, the only creature capable of harmoniously relating to Eva according to the canons of a love that alternates between courtly and romantic, codes that are precisely suited to a woman-angel plunged into Bontempelli's post-futurist literary universe. In *Siepe a nordvest* and *Eva ultima*, we come to a puppet that has surpassed the human, no longer just a bitter reminder of the search for vitality and freedom, but the highest representation of these virtues. The puppet shows this terrible and awesome power in a significant passage of the novel where Eva is seized by the desire to touch his strings and reach the metaphysical sources of erotic experience, which can be read here as a desire to know the roots of humanity.

—Miss. Eva, touch my threads.
Eva was beside herself with dismay: she yearned, tormented by a hundred desires; but with a voice made suddenly dim, she said:
—Don't tempt me.
Bululù, with great courtesy, insisted:
—Come closer, please.

[13] Ibid., 182.

[14] Ibid., 201. A few years later, in another text dominated by a female protagonist, *Minnie la candida* (*Minnie the Innocent*, 1927), Bontempelli uses the metaphor of the robot instead of the puppet to emphasize the falsity of modern existence.

Eva, as if fascinated, approached him, almost without steps, and murmured:

—Here I am about to die or go crazy.

—Closer, said Bululù, -closer... up... but slowly, please.

Eva closed her eyes, unable to resist the terror, and raised her arms, unable to resist the monstrous temptation. She groped a little with her hands, her entire body staggering; she groped over Bululù's head, and suddenly she gave a scream and drew back her hand as if she had felt it burn, and with her whole body, she jumped back and opened her eyes again.[15]

The novel contains memorable descriptions of the subtle dynamics that straddle dismay and exhilaration, inherent in discovering a harmonious relationship between the animate and inanimate. The puppet metaphor is extended widely with complexities and nuances that put *Eva ultima* on the level of artificial intelligence fiction, such as the human-operating system romance of Spike Jonze's 2013 film *Her*.[16] Bululù's appearance has a profound influence on the characters' thinking and perception. Evandro, a shrewd mind, is prompted to reflect on the soul as the "awareness of playing a role,"[17] while Eva, a sensual and emotional creature, has an allegorical hallucination in which she sees the ghosts of her loved ones in procession, overtaken by an infinity of threads of which they are unaware.[18] Moreover, for Eva, the arrival of Bululù impacts her level

[15] Ibid., 172–173.

[16] Previously Spike Jonze had collaborated with Charlie Kaufman, another influential force in experimental American filmmaking, at the making of *Being John Malkovich* (1999), a metaphysical dark comedy where a young puppeteer is drawn into a plot fraught with sex and power games by being given the opportunity of controlling a famous actor's body from within his mind. As further testament of how cinematic avant-garde draws on puppetry techniques and the puppet figure, Charlie Kaufman went on to co-direct the stop-motion tour de force *Anomalisa* (2015), with Duke Johnson, a film that stands as a most poignant example of the puppet's ability to express the fragility of selfhood in modern times through corporeal metaphors that harken back, perhaps unwittingly, to atmospheres from Bontempelli and de Chirico.

[17] Ibid., 141.

[18] The passage goes like this: "All of a sudden she seemed to see the dull air rushing from the sky in a kind of oblique, rigid rain over the heads of the larvae, who did not seem to notice it: and that mass of threads occasionally collapsed. As the threads collided with each other in this way, she thought they were about to make some sound: she waited anxiously for it, but nothing could be heard in infinite space except that frozen and buried silence throughout the earth" (ibid., 149). A little earlier, Eva and Evandro argue about

of perception, as demonstrated by the poetic descriptions of the land-scape in the moments before and after Bululù's apparition: "the whole atmosphere appeared striped by the threads of rain that crossed the space obliquely and descended rigidly to disappear without a downpour on the ground"[19] and again "Eva realized that the air of the whole room was full of a shining tremor, as above iron when red-hot or above burning sands."[20]

Bontempelli's stylistic operation parallels the method exercised by Giorgio de Chirico, who incorporates and reinvents classical aesthetics to express modern sentiments and ideas. The fact that Bontempelli turned to the ancestral version of the automaton—not only in relation to futurism but also to the source text of Ève future—thus replacing it with the puppet is certainly an indication of his broader cultural project of recon-necting with and transforming tradition, here that of puppet theater, in line with the Fascist party's need to dilute futurist experimentalism.[21] This intermediate position between modernity and tradition is in harmony with the sudden fall in tone from the lyrical to the prosaic, in the ironic desecration of the supernatural, and the friction between the psycholog-ical novel and the popular fable. While remaining politically reactionary, Bontempelli's writings retain a charge of vigorous vision and offer us a fascinating example of remediation, demonstrating the use of traditional popular theater within a reactionary avant-garde theatrical and literary operation. With exquisitely Italian traits, Bontempelli weaves a discourse of great sensitivity and innovation through the filter of the puppet and around the theme of the humanity of the machine and the painfully and inevitably platonic love between human and android.

It was then up to the creative syncretism of an artist like Federico Fellini to reconnect distant philosophical traditions and cultural genealo-gies within a bitterly ironic perspective. In Il Casanova by Federico Fellini (1976), Casanova, a guest at the court of a German prince, meets a

---

Bululù's existential status, resulting in definitions such as "God's grandchild" (as a creature of a creature of God) or "more than nothing" (as conscious of being nothing) (ibid., 126–128). When Bululù mentions his "mechanical passivity," Eva responds that the word mechanical in his case does not clarify, instead it makes one more confused (ibid., 131).

[19] Ibid., 105.

[20] Ibid., 117. Regarding the use of synaesthesia in Eva ultima see also Antonio Saccone, Massimo Bontempelli. Il mito del '900 (Naples: Liguori, 1979), 84.

[21] M. Bontempelli, L'avventura novecentista (Florence: Vallecchi, 1938), 94–95.

mechanical dancer, Rosalba, played by the dancer Leda Lojodice (1943–). The female automaton inspires great admiration in Casanova, who calls the inventor who built her "a genius, but also a poet" for having given shape to a perfect incarnation of the courtly woman, humbly resigned to exist in formulas of preordained behaviors and gestures. The character of the mechanical doll may indeed be an idealized woman, like Galatea and Ève, but if so, she resides only in the mind of Fellini's Casanova, a character unable to see beyond the cold and egocentric dream of his own male performance. In fact, the film closes with the sweet nightmare of the great Venetian lover, reduced to an emptied mannequin, a repetitive automaton, a dancing carillon doll imprisoned, together with his Rosalba, in a self-referential rotating movement.

CHAPTER 6

Adults' War in Children's Dreams: Animated Toys and Pulcinella

Abstract This chapter examines the connection between childhood and puppets in profound terms—that is, in its implications in the areas of primal drives, power dynamics, and miniaturization. The analysis focuses on how the puppet image is employed within sequences relating to a child's dream of a toy war in an early stop-motion animation film, *Il sogno e la uerra di Momi* (1917), to criticize the uncontainable destructiveness and folly of World War I. The Neapolitan puppet of Pulcinella functions as the outlet of anxieties and fears linked to conflicts among parents and the trauma of divorce for the child protagonist of *I bambini ci guardano* (1944), opening a window onto Pulcinella's association with minority struggles and social issues.

Keywords Puppets · Italian puppetry · Italian cinema · Animated toys · War · Trauma · Divorce · Childhood · Pulcinella · WWI · Vittorio De Sica · Segundo de Chomón

There certainly exists a strong association between puppet theater and the sphere of childhood; however, this is not only in terms of puppets being a form of entertainment meant primarily for a young audience. The cases that appear in this study all confirm the weight of the themes and issues that are tied to the simulacrum and the animated object, which

F. Pacchioni, *The Image of the Puppet in Italian Theater, Literature and Film*, https://doi.org/10.1007/978-3-030-98668-1_6

extend beyond, in their appeal, the realm of child spectatorship. The profound reasons puppet theater and childhood are intertwined are not always known. The puppet partakes in the domain of the *child* because it is phylogenetically linked to human childhood, considering that the practices of animating objects are rooted in the sphere of ritualism, or more precisely of symbolic thinking, in its more or less conscious forms. On this point, it should be remembered, even if in passing, how puppet theater performs religious functions in numerous Asian cultures, mixing comedy and ritual in different degrees, from the more mundane Indonesian *wayang* to the more markedly hieratic Chinese puppet theater.[1] The puppet is also *little* in the quest for miniaturization that has always marked this specific art form, the pursuit of imitation and reproduction of human life in its complexity (consider the double meaning of the name that Podrecca gives to his company, Teatro dei Piccoli [Theater of the Little Ones]). Finally, the puppet is politically and socially *small*, insofar as it is marginalized and oppressed, because of its being heir to the comedy of the *zanni*, and for being a type of theater that has lost, in its classical form, much of its social role owing to the economic, urban, and media transformations that have characterized the end of the second millennium.

Just as the emphasis on puppet theater should not be understood today as an abandonment to infantilism, the use of the image of the puppet in literature or cinema does not confine a text to an infantile audience, not even in cases where this reference directly intersects with youthful issues. In addition to the emblematic case of *Pinocchio*, there are lesser-known examples that, by uniting the sphere of childhood with the expressive effects of object animation, manage to touch a wide array of thematic chords. The fascinating way Italian cinema has reworked the substratum of figurative theatrical traditions concerning youth issues shows the great critical value of this intermedial relationship on the psychological and social level. It is a guiding thread that extends without losing its vitality, as demonstrated by two pioneering films that also mark the beginning of specific cinematic genres: the first Italian animated film *La guerra e il sogno di Momi* [The War and Dream of Momi], directed by Segundo de Chomón in 1917, one of the most refined reflections on the First World

---

[1] Particularly symptomatic of the hieratic value that the puppet theater has had in China is the testimony of Kristofer Schipper contained in the chapter "The Masters of the Gods," in *The Taoist Body* (Rome: Astrolabio Ubaldini, 1983), 57–59 (first publication: *Le Corps Taoïste. Corps Physique, Corps Social* [Paris: Fayard, 1982]).

War; as well as one of the first neorealist films, *I bambini ci guardano* (*The Children Are Watching Us*), directed by Vittorio De Sica in 1944, capable of mixing realism and psychological depth.

In 1917, Segundo de Chomón (1871–1929) wrote with Giovanni Pastrone the story of *La guerra e il sogno di Momi*, which he then scripted and directed also curating special effects.[2] The Spanish artist Chomón—a specialist in superimpositions, miniatures, and animation—spent his most fruitful period in Italy from 1912 to 1926 as a special effects director for Pastrone's films, producing with him some of the most innovative films of the silent era, including the already discussed *Cabiria*. Indeed, Chomón's work represents a striking example of the international scope of intermedial dynamics and how this artistic and cultural phenomenon unfolded in Europe across national borders.[3]

The evocative potentiality inherent in the mannequin and the man-object, explored in those same years with unforgettable effectiveness by the metaphysical art of Giorgio de Chirico and by French surrealism, can be considered a further expression of this intermedial relationship with puppet theater in the broadest sense. Already some time previously, in the film *El Hotel Eléctrico* [The Electric Hotel, 1908], Chomón had shown a particular inclination for what today would be called object performance to express the danger inherent in excessive reliance on technology, animating in stop-motion the furnishings of a hellish hotel where invisible electric currents control everything. Later, with *La guerra e il sogno di Momi*, he again employed the stop-motion technique as an expedient to create the illusion of living toy puppets, explicitly expressing the aesthetic influence of puppetry.[4]

---

[2] In 1923, Chomón also wrote and directed *Lulu*, a playful animated film of lesser importance for our study. These details are contained in the volume by Claudia Giannetto and Enrico Montrosset (eds.), *Omaggio in Musica a Segundo de Chomón* (Torino: Museo Nazionale del Cinema, 2012).

[3] Chomón also influenced one of the fathers of animated cinema, the Frenchman Emile Cohl (1857–1938). See P. Cherchi Usai, op. cit., pp. 12–13.

[4] Stop-motion originated in 1896 as a photographic trick discovered by French magician and later filmmaker Georges Méliès. It was apparently discovered accidentally: during a day of live street shooting, Méliès' camera jammed for a moment; the result was a film in which a bus seemed to be suddenly replaced by a horse. Méliès later used the trick intentionally: the transformation of the pumpkin into a carriage in his *Cinderella* (1899) is particularly well known. Here it is also worth mentioning Wladyslaw Starewicz, director of the Museum of Natural History in Kovno, Russia, who began to film scenes with

The animation of toy puppets has always traditionally linked cinema to the spheres of the marvelous and therefore to the dreamy dimension of childhood, all the way to the commercial success of Pixar's *Toy Story*, the first feature film in digital animation, where the stylization of the animated toy makes up for the still-limited refinement of the effects. It was the American company Vitagraph that first brought animal toys to life in the film *Humpty Dumpty Circus* (1897), while a few years later Edwin S. Porter made teddy bears move in *The Teddy Bears* (1907) and Arthur Melbourne Cooper animated a group of toys in *A Dream of Toyland* (also known as *Dreams of Toyland* or *In the Land of Nod*, 1907). Chomón and Pastrone clearly took up the idea of combat between animated toys within a child's dream already contained in Cooper's *A Dream of Toyland*, but also, as critic Antonio Costa notes, from Georges Méliès's *Conte de la Grand'Mère et Rêve de l'Enfant* (also known as *Au Pays des Jouets*, 1908).[5] Unlike these films, in *La guerra e il sogno di Momi*, the dreamlike value of animation flows into a critique of war. Whereas the tricks of the optical games of Mèliés are based on a comedic effect where the animated object and the optical game are meant to stimulate wonder, which for him represents the main aesthetic outcome,[6] the animated toys conceived by Chomòn are instead employed with a reflexive and demystifying function, artifices that unveil, accuse, and mock the folly of war.

The film begins with scenes in live acting where little Momi and his family, safe in their upper-class urban home, are reading a letter aloud together from the father, who is currently serving at the front line. The film cuts to the story of another child, Berto, narrated in the letter, whose life was interrupted and threatened by the military conflict unfolding near his home. While Berto directly experiences the terror, despair, and violence of war, little Momi experiences them indirectly through retellings and imagination. Indeed, especially in the second part of the film, the

---

insects, modeling their bodies, to the point of filming peculiar fairy tales such as *The Revenge of the Cameraman* (1912) and *The Grasshopper and the Ant* (1913), and later *The Story of the Fox* (1930) and *The Mascot* (1933), which were also shown in Europe. See Neil Pettigrew, *The Stop-Motion Filmography: A Critical Guide to 297 Features Using Puppet Animation* (Jefferson, N.C.: McFarland, 1999), 9–10. In Italy, see also the case of the stop-motion puppet film by filmmaker Sicilian Ugo Saitta, *Pisicchio e Melisenda (Teste di Legno)* (1937).

[5] Antonio Costa, *La morale del giocattolo: saggio su Georges Méliès* (Bologna: CLUEB, 1989), 126–127.

[6] Ibid., pp. 155–159.

Fig. 6.1 Screenshot from *La guerra e il sogno di Momi* (dir. Segundo de Chomón, 1917), DVD

horrors of war emerge thanks to a highly calculated series of scenes in stop-motion from Momi's dream. After hearing the letter, Momi turns to play, simulating a small-scale conflict with two toy soldiers, Trick and Track (Fig. 6.1); he soon falls asleep and begins dreaming. In Momi's oneiric fantasy, the toy puppets continue their conflict, escalating from a minor skirmish to an increasingly destructive mobilization of armies and stunning weapons.

The film achieves considerable depth in expressing the child's psychic world, and at the same time, in dealing with the theme of war. The fact that war is represented within the context of a child's dream indeed invites an anti-military critical perspective, as the young mind is caught in the attempt to process an immense and confusing trauma. A similar dynamic returns in other films closer to our times such as *Il cielo cade* (*The Sky Will Fall*, dir. Andrea and Antonio Frazzi, 2000) and *El laberinto del fauno* (*Pan's Labyrinth*, dir. Guillermo del Toro, 2006). However, it is the language of object animation, in its mechanistic quality and miniaturization, that allows the maximum expression of a critical and rather novel discourse about war.

The animation technique directed by Chomón fully expresses the madness of war, which leads to inventions such as the Kolossal cannon, the first chemical weapon represented in a film, presented here as an "all-machine" and of complicated management, something that the toy soldier Track transforms into a war instrument through a malign intelligence described as deriving from the mixing of alcohol and science (images 16 and 17).

Little Momi dreams of numerous war inventions, such as a giant bellows to suck chemical gases into sacks that are then returned to the sender, but also air conflicts, the bombing of the city of Lilliput, the rescue truck, and so on. More than in other war films produced by Itala Film in that period, such as *La paura degli aeromobili nemici* [The Fear of Enemy Aircraft] (1915) and *Maciste Alpino* [Hercules Mountaineer] (1916), in *Momi*, the war is seen from a bird's-eye view thanks to the detached interpretation of the human being offered by the puppet. This perspective inevitably leads to a more radical and global critique of the war phenomenon. Thanks to the animated toy, the atrocity, futility, immaturity, and senselessness of the conflict, which tramples on human bonds and destroys civilization and the environment, can be more strongly understood.

Taking a temporal leap of about thirty years and moving into a different production context, we can discover parallels between *La guerra e il sogno di Momi* and a film such as *I bambini ci guardano* by Vittorio De Sica. In both films, the puppet allows for the staging of the psychological process of the child to understand and criticize the nature of the adult social world that surrounds and conditions children. The juxtaposition of two films that are artistically and historically distant from each other reveals an interesting closeness between the expressive instruments typical of avant-garde experimentation and those of cinematographic realism. Both films use the animated puppet to reach a greater narrative depth, digging into the child's psyche; it is not by chance that the surrealist afflatus of the puppet also occupies the oneiric space of the child Pricò in De Sica's film, this time not through stop-motion but Pulcinella's theater.

Within the narrative fabric of *La guerra e il sogno di Momi* and *I bambini ci guardano*, animated puppets embody and express the trauma experienced by children. However, in De Sica's film, the trauma is no longer that of military conflict, rather it is the war between parents themselves, a conflict that deprives children of the necessary affective certainties and that exploits them within the games of revenge and guilt between spouses. *I bambini ci guardano*, based on the novel *Pricò* (1931) by Cesare Giulio Viola, follows little Pricò's ordeal during the painful events

Fig. 6.2   Screenshot from *I bambini ci guardano* (dir. Vittorio De Sica, 1941), DVD

that lead to the dissolution of his family, the suicide of his father owing to his wife's adultery, and his final abandonment in a boarding school.

The first important sequence of the film shows Pricò dragging his mother by the hand through a Roman park toward a Pulcinella show. On the small stage, we observe a love triangle between puppets: Pulcinella defends his right over signorina Gabriella and tries to intimidate a rival suitor, who, however, does not give up and challenges Pulcinella to a duel; the clash is concluded in a few moments with a flurry of beatings and with Pulcinella, the winner, dancing with his love conquest, Gabriella. In reality, such a representation is historically faithful to the repertoire of this type of puppet theater, not only regarding the show itself but also to the representation of the audience, which, in the film, is shown to be made up of adults and children who are equally interested and amused (Fig. 6.2).

Over the years, countless testimonies have been given about the trickster quality of Pulcinella, an antiauthoritarian and anarchic mask as well as a catalyst of fears and deep desires. The stubbornness, cunningness, and aggressiveness of Pulcinella's rebellious spirit in the face of devastating and humiliating attacks are only but accentuated in his incarnation as a glove puppet, a form of theater that has its roots in the sphere of the *zanni* and, as we have seen, in the most unfortunate among them, the character of Burattino. For Italian directors, Pulcinella has often been the emblem of theatrical representation as a metaphor of social history and class struggle, the banner of art that is socially committed to giving space to the suffering of minorities and the oppressed. These are the positions intensely expressed by Roberto Rossellini's voluminous and unrealized screenplay *Pulcinella o le passioni, le corna, e la morte* [Pulcinella or Loves, Betrayals, and Death] (written with Jean Gruault in the period probably starting from 1970 and ending in 1987) and by the film loosely based on it, *L'ultimo Pulcinella* (*The Last Pulcinella*, 2008), directed by Maurizio Scaparro. Let us take a brief detour to better clarify the significance of Pulcinella in a cinematic context, before returning to De Sica's film.

Rossellini's screenplay deserves particular attention because it is a clear and eloquent example of Pulcinella's revolutionary value. In this story, set in seventeenth-century Naples during the revolt of Masaniello (1620– 1641), a painter named Michelangelo inherits the mask of Pulcinella from an old and honored comedian, presented to him not only as an instrument "to always tell the truth," but as the truth's symbol.[7] After having assisted the tragic end of Masaniello, Michelangelo escapes with a group of actors, traveling the peninsula northward to reach the court of Louis XIV in Paris. Here, spurred by the Sun King to stage a representation full of artifices that may culminate in the apotheosis of the monarchy over the republic (where Tarquin violating Lucretia should be the emblem of the ideal world), Michelangelo decides, faithfully to the character of his mask, not to do as he is told and instead replaces the ending with an invective against the injustices perpetrated by those in power.

The moral legacy of the popular theater of Pulcinella concerns the defense of minority rights and of the weakest, a vocation that is strongly expressed in Rossellini's script and that has been picked up by director Maurizio Scaparro in his *The Last Pulcinella*. In Scaparro's work, Massimo Ranieri plays a traditional Neapolitan actor who insists on carrying on the tradition of Pulcinella in modern times and who travels to Paris to follow his son. There, the actor becomes involved with a group of young activists who occupy an abandoned theater and begin producing a show that applies Neapolitan comedy to the racial and class tensions experienced by immigrants in the suburbs of the European metropolis. Building on the international perspective of a transcultural Pulcinella, already contained in

---

[7] Roberto Rossellini and Jean Gruault, *Pulcinella o le Passioni, le Corna e la Morte*, "Filmcritica," May to June 1987, p. 272.

Rossellini's script, in *L'ultima Pulcinella*, the mask offers to the different Mediterranean cultures represented in the Parisian youth the possibility of peacefully channeling their demands for justice and to inspire humanity and compassion in the police to avoid violence.

Even a director such as Sergio Leone (1929–1989) recalled, more than once, the formative importance of the Pulcinella shows he saw as a child in the park of Gianicolo in Rome, dwelling precisely on the metarepresentational point of view internalized thanks to spectating such shows, as reported in 1976, in one of his interviews:

> I remember one late afternoon while returning from Trastevere. I passed by a puppet theater that was closing at that very moment [...]. From behind the lowered curtain came voices and the sound of objects being slammed here and there. Looking behind the theater, I saw the puppeteer and his wife bickering. It was a friendly quarrel and very Neapolitan. But I was struck to see the two of them hitting each other with sticks and throwing puppets at each other after the beating of the puppets on the stage [...]. As I watched that bizarre event, I understood, in my childish way, that there were things as they appeared and things that happened *behind* what appeared. Fiction and reality. There was the fairy tale of theater and the human theater, which was more serious, harsher, viler, and even more pitiful. I had just acquired my first lesson in the meaning of the word "spectacle." And that was before I even went to the movies.[8]

This quarrel between puppeteers suggests how much puppet theater has inspired reflections on the relationship between truth and representation, continuing to cast its shadow on the cinema of two great directors such as De Sica and Leone. It would then be the shadows of the *Ramayana* of an Indonesian theater (operated by Indonesian and Dutch puppeteers) that would open a key sequence of Leone's last film, *Once Upon a Time in America* (1984), alluding, as the critic Christopher Frayling notes, to the film's critical distance from the mythology of the gangster genre (the protagonist, Noodles, seems to find in the mythical space of the shadow theater a moment of escape from the contradictions and complexities of his daily life).[9]

---

[8] This quote comes from Christopher Frayling, *Sergio Leone: Something to Do with Death* (London: Faber and Faber, 2000), 8, who in turn quotes it from an interview with Noël Simsolo, *Conversations avec Sergio Leone* (Paris: Cahiers du Cinéma, 1999), 2–22.

[9] Ibid., pp. 422, 452.

Even without acquiring the gnoseological value that Plato associated with shadows in the myth of the cave, the lightning-fast and impulsive irrationality that characterizes the puppet Pulcinella is an attempt to achieve emancipation from trauma shared by the subordinate and oppressed classes: as in the case of Neapolitan people or, in *I bambini ci guardano*, of children. Returning to De Sica's film, the entire opening scene with Pulcinella's performance in the park is imbued with tensions and bitterness. When Pulcinella starts beating his rival, the camera frames the amused grinning of the older children and a crying baby, who cannot yet understand the dramatic and comedic reasons for the violence. At the same time, we see the mother of the baby, who rejects the child's instinctive reaction instead of consoling the little one and forces him to continue watching the show. In the same scene, we move immediately to the interior of the theater where the puppeteers, an eccentric couple (curiously recalling the one in Leone's memories) angrily demand the attention of a young helper, probably their daughter, scolding her and calling her stupid for not having come out promptly with the basket to collect the offering. In moments that are supposed to be festive and entertaining, violence against children might seem paradoxical were it not for the fact that this scene exemplifies the film's central theme: the violent fallout of a couple's conflicts at the expense of their child. The opening sequence and the entire film are a denunciation of the adult world, of its inability to notice and respect the needs of children.

This explicit reference to Pulcinella's theater, positioned at the film's beginning, expresses its structural function. However, the puppets reappear at another juncture, at the moment of the greatest excavation in Pricò's subjectivity, when, returning from a brief and challenging stay at his grandmother's house, Pulcinella surfaces in Pricò's hallucinated dream after he has fallen prey to fever and remorse. However before examining the child's dream, it is worth remembering some elements of the plot that precede this scene. During the night spent at his grandmother's house, the little boy wakes up intrigued by the voices of Pauline, a young girl of the house, and her boyfriend, who are meeting furtively in the garden; Pricò, looking out onto the balcony, unintentionally hits a vase that strikes the girl and abruptly turns the secret amorous moment into a scandal, and the object of the child's innocent curiosity into something tragic. In the morning, Pricò is the victim of his grandmother's fury, a woman who never misses an opportunity to express her contempt for Pricò's adulterous mother and who equally rejects the child.

Later, Pricò, while traveling back home on a train and being in the grip of a fever, has a dream. In this sequence, the accident to the detriment of Paolina and the conjugal drama of her parents are united in a theater of objects of surrealist ascendancy, in the alternation of vases, glasses, crosses, and puppets. In a particularly expressive moment of the hallucinatory dream, Pricò imagines Pulcinella beating his rival and his beloved Gabriella fiercely. The theatrical reference in the film thus becomes entirely implicit, fused, and instrumental to the language of cinema. This scene, which superficially seems to refer only to a state of confusion in the child, expresses a clear symbolic interpretation of the circumstances he is experiencing. On the one hand, there is the violence that the child now perceives as indissolubly linked to the sphere of passionate love; on the other, the delusional hope that the Pulcinella/father will punish the mother and her lover, thus bringing order back into the family as symbolized by the cheerful conciliatory dance toward which the dream progresses.

If the animated toy soldiers in *La guerra e il sogno di Momi* stage the representation of the First World War through the grotesque and at the same time humanly sincere lens of the child's imagination, the references to Pulcinella's show in *I bambini ci guardano* stage the charge of violence contained in the conflicts of couples and the impact they have on the child's psyche. Although in different ways, both the animated toy and the puppet allow for an exploration into the child's perspective and express sharp and focused criticism of adult society.

The use of intermedial practices between cinema and puppet theater, or object animation, to develop themes related to child maltreatment is by now an internationally acquired canon. This is confirmed not only by striking cases such as *Toy Story* (1995) by Pixar but also by lesser-known films such as the short film *The Wholly Family* (2001) by director Terry Gilliam (1940–), an artist who has always been very sensitive to Italian theatrical and film culture. In this last film, a child who suffers from being the scapegoat for his parents' unhappiness seems to find salvation by stealing a Pulcinella statuette.[10] At night, the statuette comes

---

[10] Although rarely acknowledged, Terry Gilliam played a crucial role in creating a particular cinematic language of surreal humor, starting with the memorable silhouette animation scenes in the *Monty Python* films. It is this style of animation that was later picked up by artists such as Trey Parker and Matt Stone for the satirical *South Park* series (where the silhouettes are then produced digitally); it is precisely the surreal charge that

alive and draws the child into a nightmare dominated by countless fright-
ening Pulcinellas, a dream centered on the nexus between physical and
emotional hunger expressing the child's loneliness and frustration. During
the dream, the child suddenly sees himself transformed into a mechanical
doll, right when his parents, after an argument, get tired of his crying
and throw him to the ground, breaking him. Through the performance
of the object (here realized with digital effects), a further symbolic passage
takes place that reveals the fundamental problem that was also Momi
and Pricò's, their feeling like impotent puppets, prey to the violence of a
war that is bigger than them. The coexistence of ancient traditions and
modern family problems, at the basis of Chomón's pioneering film and
De Sica's masterpiece, is fatalistically evoked by Gilliam in the final scene,
when the family is magically petrified into a nativity scene piece, on sale
together with the Pulcinella statuettes in the streets of Naples.

led them to return to the roots of animation by adopting stop-motion in the film *Team
America: World Police* (2004).

CHAPTER 7

The *Pupo* and the Theater of History: A Rossellinian Parenthesis

Abstract This is the first in a series of chapters highlighting the interme-dial and cinematic use of the southern form of the popular Italian puppet theater, the *opera dei pupi*. The chapter focuses on the Neapolitan episode of Rossellini's neorealist masterpiece *Paisà* (1946), in which a drunk and emotionally disturbed African American GI steps onto the stage of a *pupi* show to defend a black soldier, who, as the traditional repertoire dictates, is a Saracen who is engaged in a duel with a Christian knight. The quixotic trope of the absurd fight against the marionette and the confusion of fiction and reality underpinning it, which returns in other Italian films, speaks to the ability of the *pupo* to raise issues pertinent to the individ-ual's relationship to history; here, this ability is used in a transnational sense.

Keywords Puppets · Italian puppetry · Italian cinema · Roberto Rossellini · Neorealism · Opera dei pupi · History · *Paisà* · *Don Quixote* · Miguel de Cervantes · Marginalization · Allied bombing of Naples · Childhood · Racism

The *pupo* is the main form of puppet theater in southern Italy, with distinctive differences between the types from Palermo, Catania, Apulia, and Naples. An ancient type of marionette manipulated by a few wires

F. Pacchioni, *The Image of the Puppet in Italian Theater, Literature and Film*, https://doi.org/10.1007/978-3-030-98668-1_7

and metal rods, the *pupo* is chiefly marked by the staging of an epic-chivalric repertoire based in part on nineteenth-century compilations of Italian Renaissance poems, especially Ludovico Ariosto's *Orlando furioso* (*The Frenzy of Orlando*, 1516–1532), and in part on the tradition of the *cuntastorie*, which dates back, according to the scholarship of Cesare Segre, to the *Chanson de geste*.[1] In addition to the chivalrous repertoire, there are also other genres such as sacred dramas, farces, and stories of brigands—a variety especially prevalent in Neapolitan *pupi* theater—where the heroic subjects alternate with comic subjects such as Pulcinella and Camorra characters.[2] It is important to remember how, among the different expressions of traditional Italian puppet theater, *opera* (or *opra*) *dei pupi* occupies a privileged space in history due to the play between historiography and fantasy typical of the epic-chivalric repertoire and Ariosto in particular. Therefore, it is no coincidence that this form of theater has inspired directors who are focused on searching for truth and historical understanding, such as Roberto Rossellini and, as we will see later, Pier Paolo Pasolini.

As we have already noted about the screenplay *Pulcinella o le passioni, le corna e la morte*, Rossellini, despite being known as a director of neore-alism, never lost his interest in theater and theatricality. If the *Pulcinella* script makes explicit the link between historical truth and popular theater within Rossellini's vision, the reference to *opera dei pupi* in the Neapolitan episode of *Paisà* (1946) presents a case of intermediality that highlights the subtlety of the dramaturgical calculation hidden in Rossellini's natu-ralism and opens up broader reflections regarding the cinematic role of the *pupo*.

The second episode of *Paisà* is set in the streets of Naples after the Allies' liberation and follows the encounter between an African American soldier, Joe, and a Neapolitan street urchin, Pasquale. The *pupi*

---

[1] Cesare Segre, *La tradizione della Chanson de Roland* (Milano-Napoli: Ricciardi, 1974). See also the wide and insightful body of scholarship by Jo Ann Cavallo about the cultural history of Renaissance epic poems, with a focus on theatrical adaptations of Boiardo and Ariosto; e.g.: "Malaguerra: The Anti-State Super-Hero of Sicilian Puppet Theater" *Achilles Orlando Quixote Ulysses. Rivista di epica* I (2020): 259–294; "L'opera dei pupi e il maggio epico" in *Archivio antropologico mediterraneo* 5.7 (2002–2004): 157–170; "The Substance of Sicilian Puppet Theater: Past and Present" in *Athenaeum Review* (Fall/Winter 2020): 139–153. See also Cavallo's multifaceted digital archive at https://edblogs.columbia.edu/eboiardo/sicilian-puppet-theater.

[2] J. McCormick, et al. *The Italian Puppet Theater*, cit., 67–71.

sequence, which has been the object of fascinating analyses based on the concept of meta-representation,[3] reveals, when observed through the lens of intermediality, new and valuable implications for understanding the connection between cultural and artistic context and the stylistic choices of the director. The sequence unites the two parts of the plot of the Neapolitan episode—Joe's state of intoxication and his return to work—and brings to fruition the profound meaning of the entire episode. In the first part, Joe wanders drunkenly through the streets of Naples and meets little Pasquale, who, after some misadventures, including a turbulent visit to the *pupi* theater, steals his boots. In the second part, Joe, sober, arrests Pasquale and brings him home to punish him, but he discovers that the child is an orphan living in extreme poverty alongside many other evacuees who are victims of the devastating bombings. At that moment, the soldier suddenly forgets the child's punishment, appears overtaken by shame and in a daze, and drives away in his jeep, almost as if fleeing.

One must remember that Naples was the Italian city that suffered the most bombardment, especially by the Anglo-Americans, with about 30,000 dead and thousands of homeless seeking refuge in the city's underground caves.[4] The soldier's final escape in the grip of mixed feelings of anger, compassion, and shame is a key scene: Joe realizes that the Allied bombing, aimed at eradicating the Nazi resistance, has nevertheless caused a tragedy (for which he also feels indirectly responsible), and this understanding supersedes his desire to punish the little thief. Moreover, the feeling of anger that assails the African American soldier is strongly exacerbated by the fact that he himself is struggling with the emotional weight of his marginalization in his country of origin—a dynamic that is highlighted and activated by the *pupi* show sequence.

Between the seemingly disparate experiences of Joe and Pasquale, there is a strong parallel that the child seems to be unaware of and that the soldier seems to have initially forgotten because of the power he temporarily possesses as a representative of the occupying army. As scholar

---

[3] Millicent Marcus, "National Identity by Means of Montage in Roberto Rossellini's *Paisan*," in *After Fellini: National Cinema in the Postmodern Age* (Baltimore/London, John Hopkins University Press, 2002), 15–38.

[4] For an account of the bombing of Naples, see the volume by Sergio Villari, Valentina Russo, and Emanuela Vassallo (eds.), *Il regno del cielo non è più venuto. Bombardamenti aerei su Napoli, 1940–1944* (Naples, Giannini Editore, 2005).

68   F. PACCHIONI

Fig. 7.1   Screenshot from *Paisà* (dir. Roberto Rossellini, 1946), DVD

Millicent Marcus acutely observes, the two characters share the fundamental condition of being outcasts: "[they] are *paesani* in the displaced
persons' camp of the permanently marginalized, of those who, by virtue
of ethnicity and class, must remain in the caves and shacks that surround
the center of true social belonging."[5] Elaborating on this perspective, we
note how it is precisely on this state of unawareness and incomprehension between the two characters that the experience of the *pupi* show acts,
setting in motion a painful awareness that brings the two characters closer
together, thus transforming their relationship. In this scene, the inebriated
Joe and little Pasquale enter the crowded theater at the very moment a
paladin of Charlemagne is praising the attack against the Saracen Moors
for defending the values of civilization and justice. Recalling a political
inverse of Don Quixote's error in which the knight attacks marionettes,
mistaking them for real Saracen soldiers, Joe loses control of himself and
goes on stage to defend the Moorish knight from Orlando (Fig. 7.1).[6]

[5] M. Marcus, *op. cit.*, 23–25.

[6] Joe's sequence at the *pupi* theater clearly echoes a moment from Miguel de Cervantes' *Don Quixote de la Mancha*, namely the scene where the knight-errant mistakes a

Joe's reaction, apparently caused by the fumes of alcohol, is actually motivated by real frustrations and the need for revenge for the racial conflict he
already knows—namely, the segregation he will return to in the United
States. The *pupi* show therefore acts as a sort of psychodrama for Joe,
stimulating in him an awareness that brings him closer to the state of
marginalization experienced by the child and determines the soldier's final
reaction.

The reference to *opera dei pupi* contained in the second episode of
Paisà once again interweaves the relationship between the adult world
and the world of children. In *La guerra e il sogno di Momi* and *I bambini
ci guardano*, the animated puppet revives fears and desires hidden in the
child; however, in this second episode of Paisà, the *pupo* acts on the mind
of the unaware adult. In this episode, the realism of the representation
of the theatrical show converges (both in reference to the public in the
theater and the scenic action) with the metaphorical function of the *pupi*
themselves. In fact, Joe, having gone on stage to fight the Paladins, is
attacked by spectators and *pupari* much smaller than him; the soldier can
therefore acquire self-awareness and recognize himself in both the Italian
child and *pupo*, understanding that he too is a victim of the inescapable
upheavals of history.

It is fascinating how a traditional aspect so rooted in local southern
Italian culture can effectively enter into dialogue with the social dynamics
of a distant society's racial tensions, as it will again be shown in a later
chapter of this book in the context of Italian American immigration.
Moreover, this case incontrovertibly exemplifies Rossellini's films' shrewd
and meticulous planning—a fact that can only reinforce doubts about the
actual incidence of improvisation in this director's work. With great skill,
a stylistic strategy as sophisticated as that of the intermedial reference is
made palpable and reveals the presence of a wide-ranging dramaturgical
network underlying the realistic effect. To increase the power and evocative depth of the film, the director here resorts to the moral legacy of
the popular Italian *opera dei pupi*. This unique traditional puppet show is
thus not only an element of everyday Neapolitan life but also a powerful

---

marionette show as real and intervenes by attacking the marionettes representing an army
of Moors. In turn, we can reasonably hypothesize that Cervantes' idea may have had
something to do with the author's long stay in Naples and Messina, where he could
have observed similar ancient forms of puppet plays. See William Byron, *Cervantes: A
Biography* (New York: Doubleday & Company, Inc., 1978).

intermediary device at the heart of the film's meaning—a strategy that unfolds in the blending of theatrical and cinematic conventions on the level of repertoire and staging. The intermedial complexities of the *pupi* show sequence in *Paisà* exemplify the mechanisms underlying the expressive power of this neorealist cinema classic and its ability to express local problems in a vernacular language, masterfully transposing them onto a universal plane.

CHAPTER 8

The *Pupo* and the Theater of Life: Pasolini's Dream

Abstract This chapter addresses the extraordinary short film by Pier Paolo Pasolini, *Cosa sono le nuvole?* (1968), where live actors impersonate pupi in an idiosyncratic adaptation of Shakespeare's *Othello*. Entering into dialogue with previous scholarship primarily investigating the film's intertextual and self-reflexive qualities (Velázquez, Pirandello, etc.), the present study introduces an in-depth analysis of the aesthetic and philosophic implications of the puppet image and reference. This intermedial dynamic is examined in terms of Pasolini's directorial choices as they relate to the *opera dei pupi*, other types of puppetry and puppet figures (including Pinocchio), and the puppet inherent in the acting style of some of the actors in the cast—especially Totò and Franco Franchi. By complementing intertextual interpretations with intermedial analysis, *Cosa sono le nuvole?* is presented as a fundamental poetic manifesto for Pasolini. It is revealed to be a film that communicates Pasolini's fatalistic but vital views of human life and art in connection to the broader cultural history of the puppet metaphor.

Keywords Puppets · Italian puppetry · Italian cinema · Pier Paolo Pasolini · Totò · Franco Franchi · Opera dei pupi · Jan Švankmajer · Luigi Pirandello · Diego Velázquez · History · Don Quixote · Cervantes

F. Pacchioni, *The Image of the Puppet in Italian Theater, Literature and Film*, https://doi.org/10.1007/978-3-030-98668-1_8

The relationship between cinema and theatricality, with particular reference to the popular theater of *pupi*, became an effective tool in the hands
of another genius of twentieth-century Italy, Pier Paolo Pasolini, notably
in his short film *Cosa sono le nuvole?* (*What Are the Clouds?* henceforth *Le
nuvole*) shot in the spring of 1967 as part of the collective episodic film
Capriccio all'italiana (*Caprice Italian Style*, 1968, including directors
Mauro Bolognini, Mario Monicelli, Steno, and Pino Zac).[1] This is one
of the most intense poetic manifestos of Pasolini's cinematographic work,
a concentrated moment of reflection on his own vision of life and art, realized thanks to a daring adaptation of Shakespeare's *Othello* combined with
the use of bizarre puppets impersonated by live actors inside a popular
theater in the Roman suburbs (Fig. 8.1).

As most critics have noted, *Le nuvole* faithfully accompanies the reflections that Pasolini was articulating in these years regarding the cinema of
poetry, even as it expresses his conception of the cinematic image as the
foundation of a visual language of great cognitive impact that is closer
to reality itself than any verbal language. The scholarship has highlighted
the film's accentuated intertextual quality in connection to the central
theme of the relationship between reality and representation. Critics have
focused on the initial quotation from the painting *Las Meninas* (1656)
by Diego Velázquez, an emblem of *mise en abîme* and self-referentiality.
By showing the painter in the act of creating the picture itself and accen-
tuating the viewer's awareness of his role as an observer, the painting

---

[1] Originally, Pasolini hoped to create his own episodic film, entitled *Che cos è il cinema?*
[What is Cinema?], in which he would have fully highlighted Totò's mask of the "melancholic clown," as critic Ennio Bìspuri aptly termed it. See Ennio Bìspuri, *Totò Principe
Clown: Tutti i film di Totò* (Napoli: Guida editori, 1997), 322. *Che cos'è il cinema?*,
which remained an unfinished project because of the death of the great actor in April
1967, would also have contained *La terra vista dalla luna* (*The Earth Seen from the
Moon*), the short film that became part of the collective film *Le streghe* (*Witches*; 1967,
together with Mauro Bolognini, Vittorio De Sica, Franco Rossi, and Luchino Visconti),
along with a third short film that was never made, entitled *Re magio randagio e il suo
schiavetto schiavo* [The Stray King and His Boy Slave]. The Velázquezian posters with the
titles of the three episodes at the beginning of *The Clouds* remain as a trace of this larger
project. Cf. Emanuela Patriarca, *Totò nel cinema di poesia di Pier Paolo Pasolini* (Firenze:
Firenze Atheneum, 2006), 135. Interestingly, shortly before *Le nuvole*, Cecilia Mangini
(1927–), a photographer and documentary filmmaker close to Pasolini himself, filmed a
brief cinematographic reportage, entitled *Brindisi 1965*; in it, a skit with modern *pupi*
is used to underline the state of oppression of the working class inside the Montecatini
petrochemical plant in Brindisi.

Fig. 8.1 Screenshot from *Cosa sono le nuvole* (dir. Pier Paolo Pasolini, in *Capriccio all'italiana*, 1968), DVD

questions the perceptual conventions of art fruition.[2] Less attention has been paid to the origins and ramifications of the intricate theatrical game operated at the level of staging. In the choice of presenting *Othello* in the form of a puppet show, however, we find the link that gives coherence to the vast network of cultural references present in the film.

[2] Based on Michel Foucault's essay on the meta-representative quality of Velázquez's painting, Alberto Marchesini underlines how the game of Russian dolls, of enigma and evasion that gives life to the painting, runs through the entire short film at various levels and allows us to construct the dream perspective in the film: Alberto Marchesini, *Citazioni pittoriche nel cinema di Pasolini* (Florence: La nuova Italia editrice, 1994), 93–106. Marchesini refers to Michel Foucault's 1966 essay, *Les mots et les choses*. This reading was further developed by Marco Antonio Bazzocchi's rich study, *I burattini filosofi: Pasolini dalla letteratura al cinema* (Milan: Mondadori, 2007), where, however, Velázquez's painting is placed within a dense network of references to literary and critical works (Cervantes's *Don Quixote* and Collodi's *Pinocchio*, but also Erich Auerbach's *Mimesis* and Karl Justi's texts). In a recent essay, Daniela Bini finds numerous points of contact with Pirandellian thought and, particularly, with *Uno, nessuno, centomila*, regarding the impossibility of separating fiction and reality and the inadequacy of words: Daniela Bini, "High and Low Art, Inadequacy of Words, and Self-Referentiality in Pasolini's *Che cosa sono le nuvole?*" *Italica*, XC, no. 2 (2013): 227–44.

Neither self-referentiality nor intertextuality is sufficient to explain this film's aesthetic and cultural nature because references straddle here different media. Through the theoretical perspective of remediation, we can better understand the relationship between the philosophical reasons and stylistic choices in the film and, thus, how the film draws on the Italian tradition of puppet theater. A detailed analysis of stylistic choices—such as the interchange of puppets and flesh-and-blood actors, the choice of performers, and the references to specific and different types of puppet theater—is therefore essential to contextualize and interpret the film. In this film, thanks to particular choices of mise en scène, the accentuated remediation allows the unveiling of reality in perceptive and sensorial terms. The phenomenon of remediation brings with it, in the words of its major theorists, "the desire to get past the limits of representations and to achieve the real," and, in this way, it claims the viewer's attention by posing "as pure experience."[3] In the exceptional case of Le nuvole, the remediation of puppetry allows for a revelation of reality not only in abstract and metaphysical terms but also in perceptual and sensory terms through radical staging choices.

It is worth remembering that the first substantial history of Italian puppetry, written by Roberto Leydi and Renata Mezzanotte Leydi in 1958, was also a manifesto of resistance to modernity and a denunciation of the extinction of the popular spirit and the death of poetry. According to Leydi, the art of puppetry, whatever its form, bestows the magical gift of evoking a sense of purity, fantasy, joy, and freedom and derives from "a long and prolonged traditional process, entailing [at] once the establishment of repertoire and experimentation, which, in its most mature manifestations, expresses the tone of the highest and most complex humanity." Puppetry also has the capacity to bring together "with astonishing ease, the most refined and sophisticated cultured spirit with the warmest and most spontaneous popular spirit."[4]

This position is certainly in agreement with the outlook of Pasolini, an artist sensitive to the uncertain destiny of the premodern cultural forms of the peninsula and to the impressions of harmony, purity, and spontaneity

---

[3] J. D. Bolter and R. Grusin, op. cit., 53–54.

[4] Roberto Leydi and Renata Mezzanotte Leydi, Marionette e burattini: Testi dal repertorio classico italiano del teatro delle marionette e dei burattini (Milano: Collana del Gallo Grande, 1958), 16, 19.

that he celebrated and wished to protect.[5] The choice of a singer like Domenico Modugno (who impersonates the garbage collector) certainly coincides with this intention because he was an artist considered capable of bringing Italian music back to its rhapsodic origins, combining the act of improvisation with composition and performance.[6] In the folk revival of the 1960s, the puppet offered Pasolini a possible meeting place between the search for a cinema of poetry and the production of a Gramscian culture that was organic to the working class, a harmony that turned out to be dramatically unsuccessful, as in many of his works.[7] The process of remediation in this film is therefore also presented as redirection and recreation of a form of traditional theater that was losing much of its social role; the film attempts to preserve this tradition and simultaneously draw expressive force from it.

More than likely, Pasolini was inspired by Erich Auerbach's idea of Shakespearean writing as capable of mixing high and low tones (as outlined in his *Mimesis*, a text dear to the filmmaker). Moreover, this intermingling of tones is also expressed through the presence of the commedia dell'arte, with its many crude allusions to sexuality (the courtship between Othello and Desdemona and between Cassio and Bianca), puns ("tantissima, tantona" and "diletto, letto"), contrast between shrewdness and obtuseness (Jago and Roderigo), and influence of typical and irreverent masks such as those of Totò and Franco Franchi. However, as understood by Leydi, the coexistence between high and low culture is more fully realized thanks to the puppet. It can suffice to consider the transformation of the character of Desdemona—played by Laura Betti, friend and collaborator of the director—from a woman of sublime nobility and sagacity to a saccharine and naive creature (filmed with a doll in her arms): not by chance Betti was also known for songs

---

[5] Other stylistic choices of Pasolini are naturally linked to this aspect, including what Patrick Rumble terms "aesthetic contamination," referring to the use of premodern visual codes (in particular, Giotto, Masaccio, Bruegel, Bosch, and the Persian and Indian Rajput miniatures). See Patrick Rumble, *Allegories of Contamination: Pier Paolo Pasolini's* Trilogy of Life (Toronto: University of Toronto Press, 1996).

[6] D. Bini, *op. cit.*, no. 90.2, 238, 243.

[7] For a discussion of the way Pasolini elaborates, in the historical context of the boom years, the idea of the organic intellectual proposed in Gramsci's *Quaderni dal carcere*, see Claudio Valerio Vettraino, "Pasolini-Gramsci: crisi e decline dell'intellettuale organico," *Critica Impura* (blog), April 17, 2012, https://criticaimpura.wordpress.com/2012/04/17/pasolini-gramsci-crisi-e-declino-dellintellettuale-organico/.

such as "Venere tascabile" ("Pocket Venus"). Thank to the magic of the puppet, the lowering of the noble, tragic, and sublime Shakespearean characters to a comic–popular level does not undermine the overall lyrical tension of Pasolini's film.

In *Le nuvole*, the human is not replaced by the puppet—as does happen, for example, in the avant-garde films of the Czech director Jan Švankmajer—but instead, it is the puppet to be replaced by the human.[8] While the former has the surreal effect of transporting the spectator into a preconscious space, the latter is a strategy of existential flavor because it emphasizes the puppet nature inherent in humanity. Pasolini's tactic is typical of the puppet metaphor, which has the effect of highlighting the limits of human consciousness and the mechanisms of history outside of our control. To avoid any confusion, it must also be noted that Pasolini employs both strategies, replacing at times the human body with its simu-lacrum but only at the moments of birth and deaths of the characters in order to establish the puppet theater as the setting. Although the souls of Jago and Othello are shown as essentially free from the characters they play on the social stage, they are nonetheless slaves to the laws of narrative, and, in the cold and distant words of the puppeteer—played by the revolutionary writer Francesco Leonetti (1924–2017)—Othello is a murderer because he "wants to kill Desdemona" and Desdemona "likes to be killed."

By showing the audience of the neighborhood theater as they confuse reality and illusion and go on stage to punish Othello and Jago, the director urges a greater awareness in the viewer of the film, that is, to a reflection on the production and fruition of art. Here, too, we are dealing with the quixotic theme echoed in the second episode of *Paisà*; however, in the audience that Pasolini' portrays there is an especially feral and irra-tional tension. Not coincidentally the bitterness of the separation between the artist and the spectator, which hovers over *Le nuvole*, bring to mind the separation between the engineer Marinetti of *Fantocci elettrici* and the fishermen who are unable to recognize the automata thrown out of the window as such; the difference, though, is that, where Marinet-ti's superiority leads to the derision of the people and the scorn of the

---

[8] Michele Guerra, "Figure e cinema," in *Il mondo delle figure. Burattini, marionette, pupi, ombre*, ed. L. Allegri and M. Bambozzi, *op. cit.*, 160.

intellectuals, Pasolini idealizes the melancholic solitude of the intellectual. The audience's disconnect from the artifice of art, and its betrayal of the director-viewer bond have a tragic note and are emphasized heavily by the mixing of puppet and human, which in turn provides a correlative of the audience's own inability to discern the difference between truth and representation. It is as if Pasolini is mourning an irremediable distance between the poet and the people.

The sense of ambiguity, already inherent in the marionette as an imitation of man, is further emphasized in this film through the alternation of puppets and actors in the flesh, an effect that was planned more systematically in the script:

> Note to production. This new puppet [Othello], like all old puppets, is simultaneously one and double in nature: that is, it is made of wood like all puppets, but it is also made of flesh and blood. It will therefore be necessary to prepare as many wooden puppets as there are actors: precisely identical. In the assembly, the real and fake puppets will be alternated according to the situation.[9]

In the film, the substitution between wooden actors and flesh actors occurs only in the moments when the births and deaths of the puppets are shown, particularly Othello's (Fig. 8.2). The film's hybridity is enhanced by Pasolini's emphasis on the puppet existing within a particular approach to acting. This is evident in the case of Totò and Franco Franchi, whose acting and mimicry methods, already containing a well-established relationship with the *pupo*, are made explicit by the addition of the marionette strings that were previously only intuited.

Totò's disarticulated gesticulation is part of an acting style that comes from the fusion of the puppet theater and the variety show that took place in Naples in the early twentieth century, exemplified by the actor Gustavo de Marco (1883–1944), known as "comico zumpo" or "l'uomo di cauccìù" ("the rubber man") for his ability to imitate the articulated

---

[9] Pier Paolo Pasolini, *Cosa sono le nuvole?*, vol. I, *Pasolini per il cinema*, ed. Walter Siti and Franco Zabagli (Milan: Mondadori, 2001), 935–36.

Fig. 8.2 Screenshot from *Cosa sono le nuvole* (dir. Pier Paolo Pasolini, in *Capriccio all'italiana,* 1968), DVD

movements of the puppet.[10] Totò had learned this contortionist technique from de Marco, though he merged it with other references to puppet theater in a more flamboyant way with his Pinocchio in *Totò a colori* (1952) and sometimes with more subtlety as in the unforgettable close-ups where he grimaces while resting his chin on his hands as if on a miniature stage. As proof of the intuitive power of the true poet's eye, Pasolini's cinema captures Totò's deepest theatrical essence right at the end of the actor's career.

On the contrary, Franco Franchi's gesticulation combines Totò with Jerry Lewis, leading him to perfect a ductile facial mode of expression characterized by what has been described as "multidirectional movements of the forehead... jaw movements... lip trembling... a technical baggage that recycles at a spectacular level centuries of renunciation, oppression,

---

[10] Totò was inspired by him, and de Marco himself recognized Totò as the heir of his technique. The influence was not only in the marionette style of the performance but also in specific sketches, among others, those of Bel Ciccillo, which Totò stole with great success from de Marco. See Ennio Bìspuri, *Vita di Totò* (Rome: Gremese, 2000), 45, and Roberto Escobar, *Totò* (Bologna: Il Mulino, 1997), 27. The case of the great actor Ettore Petrolini (Rome 1886–1936) is also part of this network of relationships, both for the acting inspiration drawn from the puppet theater (and from Italo Ferrari of Parma in particular) and for the influence he had on the young Totò; for a more detailed analysis, see A. Cipolla and G. Moretti, *Commedianti figurati e attori pupazzani, op. cit.,* 21–25.

hunger and sexual repression."[11] Franco Franchi's *pupo*-like gesticulation is fully exploited in the film *I Zanzaroni* (directed by Ugo La Rosa), which was released not coincidentally in the same year as *Le nuvole*: here, the actor exhibits his virtuosity by demonstrating, to a penniless puppeteer (Ciccio Ingrassia), whose theater is about to close for lack of an audience, how a *pupo* is supposed to move. The choice to emphasize the puppet intrinsic to Totò and Franco Franchi is an example of the phenomeno-logical excavation that Pasolini applied to the art of cinema in these years, searching for the medium's most ancient and indigenous sources to increase its vitality and poetic power further.

The film makes a theatrical reference to the Catanese-style *pupi* theater, where puppeteers work from the top of the deck rather than from the side of the stage, as is typical of the Palermo puppets. As we have seen, the acting exemplified by Totò and Franco Franchi is rooted in the movements of the *pupo*, and the military and tragic theme of *Othello* is consonant with the repertoire of this form of southern puppet theater, traditionally based on chivalry cycles. However, the film is pervaded by a ravenous inclination to integrate a significant number of references, as if to exhaust the entire metaphorical potential of the puppet both as an idea and a sensory presence. The recurring substitution of the *pupo* with the more general *burattino* in the screenplay is a symptom of Pasolini's desire to bring into play all the existential value of the puppet that takes hold, as Leydi sensitively notes, "where the last effort of expressive stylization and logical abstraction of the human body fails."[12] The claim of a new experience of reality, which, as we have seen, is a fundamental goal of the act of remediation, grows in vigor thanks to Pasolini's brilliant staging of the puppet's metaphorical qualities. For this reason, the film opens with a fleeting yet dazzling reference to Pinocchio, the rebel puppet par excel-lence—which is also the more hybrid and complete puppet—acting in the film behind the character of Othello during his creation in the opening and his gradual coming to consciousness.[13]

---

[11] Alberto Castellano and Vincenzo Nucci, *Life and Entertainment of Franco Franchi and Ciccio Ingrassia* (Naples: Liguori, 1982), 31.

[12] Leydi and Mezzanotte Leydi, *op. cit.*, 14.

[13] Pondering on the presence of Pinocchio in this film, Bazzocchi suggests that a reflec-tion on death is developed by showing Pinocchio's exit from the theater, rather than his entrance, as it occurs in Collodi's text (Bazzocchi, *op. cit.*, 96–97). We could also reflect on the anarchic value inherent in the representation of persons of short stature contained

In the script of *Le nuvole*, Othello listens for the first time to the sounds coming from the city around the theater, another mysterious world that the puppets, prisoners of the theater, do not know but sooner or later will encounter after the last performance. In fact, the two protagonists discover their true nature and behold reality itself only after their characters' demise, when they suddenly find themselves in the dump under the sky, confronted with the "heartbreakingly wonderful beauty of creation" (image 26). It is the same breaking of illusion we find in Pirandello's *Il fu Mattia Pascal* (1908), yet diametrically opposite to it. Let us recall here the famous passage in which the theosophist Anselmo Paleari shares with the protagonist Meis-Pascal the announcement of a staging of Sophocles's *Oreste* for "automatic marionette, of new invention":

"The tragedy of Orestes in a marionette theater!" Anselmo Paleari announced to me one day. "They're automatic marionettes, a new invention. It's this evening at 8:30 at 54 via dei Prefetti. It's worth going, Signor Meis."

"The tragedy of Orestes?"

"Yes, 'd'Après Sophocle,' the poster says. It must be *Electra*. Just listen to what I've just thought of! If at the climax, just when the marionette representing Orestes is about to take revenge for his father's death on Aegisthus and the mother, what if there were a tear in the sky of the paper theater, what would happen? You tell me."

"I don't know," I replied, shrugging my shoulders.

"But it's easy Signor Meis! Orestes would be disconcerted by that hole in the sky."

"Let me tell you. Orestes would still feel inclined to revenge and would want to carry it out with maniacal passion, but, just as he was about to do it, his eyes would be drawn to the hole, from which all kinds of adverse influences would penetrate the stage, and his avenging arm would fall. Orestes in fact would turn into Hamlet. Believe me, Signor Meis, the whole difference between ancient and modern tragedy consists in just that, a hole in a paper sky!"[14]

---

in *Las Meninas* because, in the seventeenth-century court, they represented, as jester-like figures, an accepted element of disorder and the freedom of expression.

[14] Luigi Pirandello, *The Late Mattia Pascal* (Sawtry: Dedalus, 1987), 145 (first edition of the original: Rome, "Nuova Antologia," 1904). The quotation also contains an ironic reference by the author to the pseudoscientific poses of the theatrical performers of the time.

Here, Paleari suggests the reason for the reaction of Oreste's marionette to the sudden bursting of the paper sky of the theater's scenery; in doing so, he explains that the difference between ancient and modern tragedy (with reference to Shakespeare's *Hamlet*) lies precisely in the breakdown of an illusory conception of reality. Even if Paleari's abstraction is humorously lowered by the irony of the language and circumstances in which his words are dropped, Paleari's observation falls into the modernist groove of Pirandello's text, where Pascal's migrations through different lives and identities act as an analogy to relativism in broader terms. This is a further fracture in the classical Western *forma mentis*, already made explicit by the second preface of the novel in Pascal's invective against Copernicus for having disturbed the happy ignorance of men by placing them in front of a cosmic infinity in which the earth is but "a grain of crazed sand."[15]

The anguish of Pirandello's puppet confronted with the hole in the sky is replaced in *Le nuvole* by the wonder of Pasolini's puppet faced with the unknown. In this context, in *Le nuvole* (but also in the previous *The Earth Seen from the Moon*) the end of life is optimistically seen as a moment of liberation from the damnation of history, as a moment of truth in relation to Pasolini's conception of film editing as a conclusive gesture that suddenly gives meaning to a story: "Death performs a lightning montage of our life... only thanks to death does our life serve to express us."[16] Pasolini's poetic perspective on death, however, also underlies the link that this film sustains, through *Othello*, with classical tragedy, both Greek and Latin.[17]

Over the course of the twentieth century, the marionette, of which the *pupo* is an archaic version, continued to develop a vitalistic line of thought with different modalities that reveal the particular interests of the

---

[15] Ibid., 18.

[16] Pier Paolo Pasolini, *Empirismo eretico* (Milan: Garzanti, 1991), 241 (first edition: 1972). The translation is mine.

[17] Death is "symbolically... the purest moment of life," writes Roland Barthes, referring to Tacitus's historical narrative, echoing an idea characteristic of classical tragedy. The idea also occurs in a text such as *Othello*, which is underlain by the conception of life as a representation understandable only at the moment when one abandons one's part. See Catharine Edwards, "Acting and Self-Actualization in Imperial Rome: Some Death Scenes," in *Greek and Roman Actors* (Cambridge: Cambridge University Press, 2002), 377–94. From the same source (page 389), I draw and translate Barthes's own words, originally in Roland Barthes, "Tacitus and the Funeral Baroque," in S. Sontag, ed., *Barthes: Selected Writings* (London, 1982), 166.

various authors. While on the one hand the marionette expresses the relativistic pessimism of Pirandello, on the other hand the *pupo,* predisposed
to the representation of history as myth and fantasy, favors a perspective
aimed at transcending and breaking illusion. Therefore, we can conclude
by comparing the Neapolitan episode of *Paisà* by Rossellini and the short
film by Pasolini. On the one hand, Rossellini's careful choice of the intermedial reference allows for the covert realization of a deep philosophical
plot within a realist style. On the other hand, Pasolini's interchange of
pupi and actors makes explicit the analogy between the puppet show and
life—and then, in a Pirandellian way, tears away the epistemological limits
without, however, falling into relativistic pessimism but rather ascending
into a vital mysticism.[18]

---

[18] The use of puppetry to evoke a greater and unknown reality beyond our perception
and understanding is at the heart of Krzysztof Kieślows's hypnotic masterpiece of cinematic
introspection and metaphysical evocations, *The Double Life of Veronique* (1991). Here it
is the character of a puppeteer, pursuing and eventually seducing the French Veronique,
who allows her, through his gift of twin marionettes in her image, to acknowledge her
secret awareness of ubiquitous existence.

CHAPTER 9

Poetry and Politics of the Emilian Puppet: Bertoluccian Memories

Abstract This chapter analyzes the aesthetic and political significance of the reference to northern Italian glove puppetry in Bernardo Bertolucci's generational film *1900* (1976). The analysis reveals the affective and artistic relationships among Bernardo; his father, the poet Attilio Bertolucci; the puppetry tradition of Emilia-Romagna, and, particularly, the Ferrari family of puppeteers, who collaborate in the film. The investigation traces the connections among left-wing politics, puppetry, and cinema in Parma. This chapter also examines how the commedia dell'arte glove puppet tradition can communicate with its audience and the broader implications of this theatrical reference in Bertolucci's cinema.

Keywords Puppets · Italian puppetry · Italian cinema · Bernardo Bertolucci · Attilio Bertolucci · Ferrari family · Preti family · Sandrone · Communism · Strikes · Oppression · Language

In the Parma countryside, during the general agrarian strike of 1908, the strikers' children are being sent to Genoa, where the Soccorso Rosso, the coordinated Communist support network, will care for them. While waiting for the train to leave, parents and children attend a puppet show

83

F. Pacchioni, *The Image of the Puppet in Italian Theater,
Literature and Film,* https://doi.org/10.1007/978-3-030-98668-1_9

Fig. 9.1   Screenshot from *Novecento* (dir. Bernardo Bertolucci, 1976), DVD

in the piazza. Though offering a moment of distraction and laughter before the separation, the performance also becomes a voice of collective resentment toward landlords and the authorities. The dialogue between the two glove puppets Fagiolino and Sandrone, the two servants on stage, underlines the unfolding strike and the reasons for the children's departure. Sandrone's blunders are countered by Fagiolino's wit, providing much comedic relief. The puppets soon begin to call for a general strike and revolution. At this point, two puppet carabinieri enter the small stage and receive a sound thrashing from the puppet servants. The scene attracts the attention of two real carabinieri on horseback, who attack the puppet theater with saber strokes, causing the indignant public to begin pelting the policemen with stones (Fig. 9.1).

The sequence described above is from Bernardo Bertolucci's film *Novecento* (1976). As happens in other films by this director, we find strong friction between the desire to tell the story of the twentieth century in a Marxist tone and the wish to evoke the past as a lost paradise through a Proustian and psychoanalytic lens. The film was harshly criticized and rejected by members of the PCI (Partito Comunista Italiano) because of its appropriation of important chapters in the history of the class struggle and its retelling of them from a distinctly bourgeois and sensual perspective.[1] Despite this, examining the sequence at the train station as a microcosm of the film's broader dynamics shows that the intermedial relationship between cinema and puppetry allowed Bertolucci to create cinematic harmony between ideology and lyricism.

The reference to a specific tradition of Italian puppetry, in this case, the Emilian glove puppets, is manifested with remarkable historical rigor. A historic family of puppeteers from Parma, the Ferrari family, stages the spectacle in the film, employing authentic puppets and set design from the beginning of the century. Bertolucci paid tribute to the puppeteers whose shows punctuated his childhood spent in Parma: "I finally had to make a film, *Novecento,* to be able to see the puppets of the Ferrari brothers! We organized a puppet show for the children who were leaving. And it was the best way actually to understand my connection with the Ferraris."[2]

The reference to puppets, which is only one of the many elements of folklore present in this film, is part of the broad revival of a popular, dialectal, and regional culture that took hold in the 1960s and 1970s in Italy. It is no coincidence that the director is particularly interested in a character such as Sandrone, who is important to the Modenese tradition that stretches from the artistic Campogalliani and Preti families to the Ferrari family. Sandrone, who, with time, ended up becoming only a side character to Fagiolino, is originally a dominant character. In the show represented in *Novecento,* we see Fagiolino's promptness and shrewdness, while Sandrone rambles without restraint; take, for instance, the lines from *lazzi* repertoire: "L'occhio del collo," "La lingua tagliata,"

---

[1] Michele Guerra, *Gli ultimi fuochi* (Rome: Bulzoni, 2010), 255–262.

[2] Interview contained in the documentary *The Puppeteers,* directed by Laura Calder and Maurizio Rigamonti, 2007.

"Il vaccabolario"). If, in the film, Olmo's grandfather, Leo Dalcò (Sterling Hayden), embodies the authenticity and obstinacy of the village, Sandrone represents its bitter destiny. Sandrone's ignorance is, in fact, understood as "not knowing what is outside of one's own ethnicity."[3] Sandrone is, therefore, the bitterly ironic personification of the decline of the peasant world, of its drifting into a grimace of increasing ridicule, of its inability to take hold of modern reality, sadly surviving within the limits of absurd comicality. As the director's interviews reveal, it was the profound humanity of this puppet that struck him when he watched the Ferraris' shows as a child; Sandrone's surprising ability to stage unexpected psychological subtleties: "One of the things that I always loved most was when Sandrone would put his hands like this [grabbing his head], and Fagiolino would say, 'What are you doing?' Sandrone would say, 'I'm thinking. I'm thinking.'".[4]

The nostalgic evocation of figures from the world of Parma's popular theater undoubtedly belongs to the Proustian spirit of the film. Moreover, in this sequence, one can trace the echo of the poem *La camera da letto* (*The Bedroom*) by the director's father, Attilio Bertolucci (1938–2000), written a few years earlier and a great, dreamy fresco that, not coincidentally, critics have described as "peasant Proustism."[5] In one passage of the poem, in chapter XV, *Nonno e nipote* (*Grandfather and Grandson*), there is an elegiac description of the childish joy of being in front of an evening puppet show.

---

[3] Remo Melloni and Paolo Parmiggiani, *I Ferrari di Parma. Storia di una famiglia di burattinai* (Parma: Monte Università di Parma, 2009), 34.

[4] Bernardo Bertolucci interviewed in the documentary *The Puppeteers*, op. cit.

[5] Gianni Pozzi, *La poesia italiana del Novecento* (Torino: Einaudi, 1970), 330. The love for the puppet theater did not spare even Bernardo's brother Giuseppe Bertolucci, who in his short film on Bologna, contained in *12 registi per 12 città* (12 Directors for 12 Cities, 1989), gave a central role to the puppets typical of the city.

I soldi che ti scottano nelle tasche infantili
– le granatine precoci non riescono a consumarli
–
oggi potrai alfine barattarli con un piacere
nuovo e misterioso: il teatro dei burattini
Lascia che termolabile già, ignaro, l'aspettazione
dell'ora lilla in cui il sole muore lentamente
sulle colline basse a corona di Salsomaggiore
e nasce ardente di fuochi e lampi la vita
di un medioevo regale e villano ti colori
la faccia d'ardore subfebbrile. Basterà
che spiando di dietro il sipario vermiglio
l'occhio rotondo di gufo avvezzo alle ore
notturne
del più anziano dei fratelli Preti conti
un numero sufficiente di tavolini occupati
perché una musica attacchi, foriera di
avvenimenti
ignoti: medicamento sufficiente a rimetterti
in equilibrio termico, a rallentare
i battiti del tuo cuore e allontanare
dalla superficie del tuo essere l'urgenza
pulsante e minacciosa della vita personale
Qui comincia l'arte, qui la finzione
si fa tempo più vero di quello che doloroso
scorrendo tocca le tue membra: amori
e duelli, suono di mandòle e di spade
interrompe e varia saviamente l'astuzia
dei servi cui soltanto è concesso
lo sfogo delle bastonate a imitazione
dei tornei e il salto delle mazurke
e polke a contrappunto degli inchini regali[6]

The money burning in your infant pockets–
the quick grenadine drinks cannot spend it all–
today you will be able at last to trade it with
a new
and mysterious pleasure: the puppet theater
Already thermolabile, unaware, let the
expectation
of the lilac hour, in which the sun slowly dies
out
over the low hills crowning Salsomaggiore
and the life of a regal and uncivil Middle Ages
is born burning with fires and lightning,
tinge your face with subfebrile ardor. It will be
enough
for the round owlish eye of the oldest of the
Preti brothers
used to the night hours, spying from behind
the vermillion curtains
to count a sufficient number of occupied tables
and a music will start, harbinger of unknown
events:
sufficient medication to reestablish
your thermal equilibrium, to slow down
the beating of your heart and to drive away
from the surface of your being the throbbing
and menacing urgency of your personal life
Here is the beginning of art, here make-believe
becomes a time more real than the one
touching your limbs in its painful course:
loves and duels, the sound of mandolas and
swords
interrupts and varies wisely the cunning
of the servants who are granted only
the outlet of thrashings in imitation
of the jousts and the leaping of mazurkas
and polkas as a counterpoint to the royal bows

[6] Attilio Bertolucci, *La camera da letto* (Milan: Garzanti, 1984), 126–127. See also the pages in which the poet recalls with affection and wonderment his childhood experiences with puppet shows, and in particular with the Ferrari puppet, defined as "the supreme spectacle," which he witnessed in the barn of his father's country house and in the cafés of Salsomaggiore. In these pages, the poet recalls the glove puppets as "people fixed in the face and so mobile in the body" and his favorite character, Sandrone, as "woody, earthy, and phlegmy" in contrast to the "flying aerial marionettes." A. Bertolucci, *Burattini e marionette* in *Opere* (Milan: Mondadori, 2012), 1193–1195. The English translation of the longer quote comes from Attilio Bertolucci, *The Bedroom*, trans. Luigi Bonaffini (New York: Chelsea Editions, 2012), 238–239.

In these verses, the puppet theater is filtered through the lens of prim-
itivism consistent with the folkloric attitude of the 1960s and 1970s. The
puppeteer, a member of the Preti *famiglia d'arte*, from which the Ferrari
family learned its skills, with his "round owlish eye... used to the night
hours," evokes the sphere of magic and fairytale. Then, the warning of
the beginning of the performance, with its imaginative music, is enough
to trigger a physical reaction, a "sufficient medication to reestablish /
your thermal equilibrium, to slow down / the beating of your heart," an
experience that allows you to escape from the worries and thoughts of
"personal life."

The relationship between spectacle and audience shown in the *Novecento* sequence under examination has historical roots. Both puppet and
marionette shows have always had an informative function in urban
centers because they integrated news about current events.[7] As evidence
of this practice, in the city of Parma, we can point to the political duets
with which the Ferraris concluded their shows during the months leading
to the referendum on the female vote in 1946; or the musical number
inspired by the friendly rivalry between the cyclists Gino Bartali and
Fausto Coppi, with which they closed their shows in the months following
the famous 1952 *Tour de France*.[8]

Communism and puppets, two key elements in the history of Parma,
intertwine in the 1970s both within and without Bernardo Bertolucci's film. In those years, the Ferraris' shows had acquired a satirical tone
toward the government, especially in their new type of performance, the
cabaret, where a puppet representing a Parma villager, Bargnòcla, is ques-
tioned by an offstage interviewer.[9] This kind of performance was well
received in Parma, a traditionally left-leaning city, and the location of
some of the most heated clashes led by student and workers' movements.
Therefore, it is not by chance that, alongside their nostalgic flavor, the
puppets in *Novecento* have ideological value. On the contrary, we can say
that the director privileges the political charge of this form of popular
theater because it reinforces, rather than exorcises, the demonstrators'
concerns. The harsh agrarian general strike of 1908 in the Parma area,

[7] Alfonso Cipolla and Giorgio Moretti, *Storia delle marionette e dei burattini in Italia*
(Pisa: Titivillus, 2011), 42, 100, 191.

[8] R. Melloni, P. Parmiggiani, *op. cit.,* 119, 124–125.

[9] Ibid., 180–181.

which serves as the backdrop for the train station sequence in *Novecento*, is one of the key moments in the history of the city's left-wing politics. In the 1970s, as the film shows, it acquired the symbolic value of a moral tradition and a historic struggle.

The local gazette welcomed the Ferraris' participation in Bertolucci's Marxist-style colossus with the enthusiasm and pride one feels when seeing something typical of a city's life immortalized in the temple of international spectacle. It is a collaboration that, in a certain sense, closes the circle that unites Parma's revolutionary soul: popular theater (i.e., low culture) and auteur cinema (i.e., high culture).

> Sandrone and Fasolino are the stars of the cinema. The "Ferrari puppets" are, in fact, in the cast of Bernardo Bertolucci's *Novecento*. Their names, which have been on screens worldwide since December 1975, are engraved on the credits next to the "greats." Next to the peasant ethos, literary references (from Fenoglio to Pavese), history, events, sociology, and so much political charge, there is a place for the wooden heads of Borgo Santo Spirito [the neighborhood where the laboratory of Giordano Ferrari was located]. There are yards of film stock dedicated to the nervous creatures of Giordano, Jimmy, and Luciano Ferrari, all leaving their "cave" at the corner of Piazzale Serventi to stand in front of the cameras. And, this time, "polenta served on a silver platter"—the well-known motto of the house—is offered to millions of spectators. The wooden actors from Oltretorrente [one of the historic neighborhoods of the city], along with the fussy Toscanini and the bubbly Verdi Chorus, stage the soul of that district, of a region; they embody a simple sincerity that never lacks directness and never disappoints.[10]

---

[10] Antonio Mascolo, "Sandrone e Fagiolino attori in 'Novecento' di Bertolucci," *Gazzetta di Parma*, Thursday, September 26, 1974, 9. Here is passage from the local gazette in the original Italian: "I burattini dei Ferrari" sono, infatti, nel cast del film di Bernardo Bertolucci "Novecento." Il loro nome, dal dicembre '75 sugli schermi di tutto il mondo, scolpito sulla colonna sonora accanto a quello dei "grandi",... Accanto all'ethos contadino, ai riferimenti letterari, da Fenoglio a Pavese: accanto alla storia, alle vicende, alla sociologia e a tanta carica politica, un posto per le teste di legno di Borgo Santo Spirito. Metri di pellicola per le nervose creature di Giordano, Jimmy e Luciano Ferrari, uscite tutte assieme dalla "grotta" all'angolo di piazzale Serventi per porsi davanti alle macchine da presa. E questa volta "la polenta servita sul piatto d'argento"—il cosiddetto motto della casa—viene offerta a milioni di spettatori... Gli attori di legno dell'Oltretorrente, a coté del pignolo Toscanini, e della spumeggiante Corale Verdi, mettono in scena, a canovaccio, l'anima di quel quartiere, di una regione. Una sincerità semplice che non arzigogola. E non delude.

With the following words, Bertolucci describes his interest in the symbiotic relationship between news events and entertainment, between the public and puppets, at the basis of the sequence in *Novecento*: "I was filming a puppet show, reproducing events unfolding in the station square.... It is as if everything was born from the puppet show and then extended its influence in reality around the small theater."[11] The director underlines puppetry's revolutionary potential by staging it as a metonymy of the strike and as the focal point of the uprising: the charge of the carabinieri is, in fact, directed first of all at the theater and is the gesture that inflames the clash. As the people's voice, the puppets suggest the possibility for the peasants to appropriate the land. Referring to the insurrectional and social quality of the glove puppet, the film confirms the vital link that has always existed between this specific form of Italian puppet theater and the commedia dell'arte, showing how this tradition, which combines actors' theater and puppetry, continued to play an essential role in the manifesto of Italian counter-culture in the 1970s.

The guards' quixotically excessive reaction could seem to be a typical 1968 representation of irrational power. However, it is historically proven that puppeteers have often been subject to censorship, to the point that scholars have found it helpful to resort to police archives to find data about the work of particular artists. On the one hand, the street puppet can serve as an effigy, as in a demonstration, to criticize and ridicule otherwise distant political figures (see, a different national context, the telling case of the Syrian company Masasit Mati); on the other hand, the political vitality of this form of theater comes from its ability to remain open to novelty, improvisation, and reformulation.[12]

Bernardo Bertolucci's intention to align himself with the sociopolitical side of the glove puppet highlights an interesting case of language fusion. The puppet show's dialogue with the audience has a narrative function: it conveys information that the film viewer needs to understand the historical events, explaining the precise reason for and destination of the departing children. The director skillfully employs the characteristic relationship between audience and puppets, not only for the remarkable

[11] Bernardo Bertolucci interviewed in the documentary *The Puppeteers*, op. cit.

[12] Another example of such characteristics and dynamics can be found in the political charge of Punch & Judy's theater in San Francisco's American counter-culture. Claudia Oreinstein, *Festive Revolutions: The Politics of Popular Theater and the San Francisco Mime Troupe* (Jackson, Mississippi: University Press of Mississippi, 1998), 54–89.

historical accuracy of this explicit theatrical reference but also implicitly employing the performance as a narrative device.

As the Italian theatrical experience of the 1960s and 1970s teaches us, in particular the work of Dario Fo (1926–2016),[13] traditional forms of popular theater, such as Pier Paolo Pasolini's Teatro di Parola, can convey complex concepts to a working-class audience better than purely intellectual forms. It is no coincidence that Pasolini, who was Bertolucci's mentor, also found a philosophical and poetic balance by approaching the world of puppet theater from the complex and ambitious overview of the life of the spirit and the limits of art in *Cosa sono le nuvole?* It is undoubtedly also due to the emphasis on psychoanalytic themes, therefore becoming more literary and mythical, that the Pasolinian Bertolucci lost contact with the mass audience at times. However, a sequence such as that of the puppet show during the strike, thanks to its intersection with a popular form of spectacle, represents a particularly felicitous moment in the film, where Marxist and bourgeois points of view seem to find a balance.

The decision to end the sequence with puppeteer Luciano Ferrari (1934–1978), who plays *L'Internationale* on an accordion as the train departs, blends the nostalgic point of view of the folklorist with the political horizon.[14] The gaze, and even more so the hollowed-out face of the eminent puppeteer, already suffering in those days from a terminal illness, communicates a "prophetic expression," according to the director, "of

---

[13] Among Italian playwrights, Dario Fo, more than others, explored the use of mannequins and marionettes in stage plays such as *Grande pantomima di pupazzi* (1968) and *Morte e resurrezione di un pupazzo* (1971), and variously demonstrated, as Christopher Cairns has lucidly analyzed, a well-established use of the puppet as an element of the actor's theatrical language. We find instances of replacing the actor with the mannequin, symbolic of the puppet, the theme of the control or construction of the puppet, the presence of the mannequin as a double or as an embodiment of elements of the psyche, and so on. These and other strategies raise political and existential issues of various kinds, leading back to Giorgio de Chirico's metaphysical mannequins, Marinetti's futurism and Pirandello's problems of identity. Furthermore, the influence of Fo's wife, Franca Rame, whose family has deep roots in the world of traditional puppetry, should not be overlooked. See the excellent essay by Christopher Cairns, "Man is Non-Man: Mannequins, Puppets and Marionettes in the Theater of Dario Fo," in *Pinocchio, Puppets and Modernity*, ed. Katia Pizzi (New York/London, Routledge, 2012), cit., 93–108.

[14] R. Melloni, P. Parmiggiani, *op. cit.,* p. 183.

hope, utopia, dream and also the sense of a condemnation" becoming "a sort of icon to the revolution."[15]

The merging of cinematic narrative techniques with street art conventions like the glove puppet implies an interest in appropriating the emancipating force that this theater has on the level of communication. In the sequence at the train station, the film makes its own "*scivolosità*" (slipperiness) that the poet Roberto Roversi (1923–2012) found in the expressive nature of puppet theater, a characteristic for which "the spectacular operation of communication develops and organizes itself while it is being carried out."[16] Thanks to this kind of quality, Roversi considers puppetry not a dead art, but a possible platform for the reconquest of communicative freedom in the fight against the authoritarian commodification of language. The intermediality contained in *Novecento* brings a revolutionary charge also on the level of communication, intertwined in this way with the sphere of poetry, in harmony with the highest ambitions of Bertolucci's artistic activism.

[15] Bernardo Bertolucci interviewed in the documentary *The Puppeteers*, op. cit.

[16] Roberto Roversi, "I burattini dopo Campoformio," in *Occhi di vetro occhi di legno*, eds. R. Roversi and M. Fincardi (Reggio Emilia: Edizioni Diabasis, 1990), 20.

CHAPTER 10

Vulgarity and Grace: Avant-Garde Echoes in Lina Wertmüller's Cinema

Abstract This chapter explains the importance of puppetry and the puppet metaphor in the cinema of Lina Wertmüller. Drawing from interviews and new archival materials, the discussion unveils Wertmüller's early collaboration with Maria Signorelli, one of the most original Italian puppeteers of the twentieth century. Signorelli's puppets, which Giorgio De Chirico and Giuseppe Ungaretti characterized as able to uplift humble materials into lyrical plasticity, are shown as analogous to Wertmüller's compassionate and satirical portrayal of human nature, where contradictions and vulgarity lead—via puppet-like choreography, acting, and makeup—to a deeper understanding of the unruly nature of the game of life and at times to human innocence and grace.

Keywords Puppets · Italian puppetry · Italian cinema · Lina Wertmüller · Apprenticeship · Federico Fellini · Maria Signorelli · Giorgio de Chirico · Bragaglia family · Socialism · Choreography · Dance · Nonverbal language · Puppets · Pedagogy

Over the centuries, in the case of many playwrights and directors, puppet theater has been an essential formative game of childhood, a fundamental exercise for its combination of invention, direction, and acting. Famous are the cases of the youthful experiences of Carlo Goldoni (1707–1793)

© The Author(s), under exclusive license to Springer Nature Switzerland AG 2022
F. Pacchioni, *The Image of the Puppet in Italian Theater, Literature and Film*, https://doi.org/10.1007/978-3-030-98668-1_10

in Vipacco, where he staged Pier Jacopo Martelli's *bambocciata* (play
for puppets), *Lo starnuto d'Ercole* (Hercule's Sneeze). As the memories of the Venetian playwright reveal, this experience with puppets was
an exercise in dramaturgy and direction: structuring the story, propor-
tioning thoughts and feelings to the characters, and understanding how
to manage the practical aspects of the theatrical machine.[1] The ancient
groove of this educational practice can also be found in recent times
and cinematographic contexts, as in the case of the Swedish director
Ingmar Bergman; who reminisces on his discovery of dramaturgy via
puppetry *Fanny and Alexander* (1982). Fellini—a model for Lina Wertmüller—deeply cherished the sensorial dimension of puppetry's artisanal
experience in connection to the visceral, meticulous, and fluid approach
to the direction of the mise-en-scene of his film. Fellini even went as far as
to pursue an approach to directing actors based on the puppeteer/puppet
model, in which the director claims total and tyrannical control over the
actor, radically altering his physiognomy, guiding his movements with
maniacal precision, and dubbing their voice.[2]

[1] In the first pages of his autobiography and in the preface of some of his comedies,
Goldoni recalls how his vocation was born from the game of puppets. This is how Goldoni
recounts his childhood games: "[My father] had a puppet theater built: he himself made
them move with three or four friends and I, at the age of four, found it a delightful
amusement." The experience of the *bambocciata* in Vipacco is described as follows: "In
order to provide me with some distraction, Count Lantieri had a puppet theater, that was
lying half-abandoned even though it was full of puppets and scenery, set up for me. I took
advantage of this and entertained the entire group of guests by staging a work by a great
author, written especially for puppet theater: it was *Lo starnuto d'Ercole*, by Pier Jacopo
Martello, from Bologna.... The author's imagination pictured Hercules in the country of
the pygmies.... There is a plan, a progression, a plot, a catastrophe, an adventure; the style
is good and well supported; the thoughts, the feelings, everything is proportioned to the
height of the characters; even the verses are short, everything, all in all, speaks of pygmies.
For the character of Hercules it was necessary to construct a gigantic puppet; everything
was executed to perfection. The amusement was much appreciated. I would bet, in fact,
that I was the only one who had the idea of staging the *bambocciata* of Signor Martello."
See Carlo Goldoni, *Memorie*, ed. Paolo Bosisio (Milan: Arnoldo Mondadori, 1993), 28,
106–107 (first edition: *Mémoires de M. Goldoni, pour servir à l'histoire de sa vie et à celle
de son théâtre*, Paris, Duchesne, 1787).

[2] See the interview with the makeup artist of *Amarcord*, Rino Carboni, filmed in the
backstage by Maurizio Mein (DVD, Criterion Collection), and the sequence of the effu-
sions between Encolpius, Ascilto, and the young foreigner in the house of the Roman
patricians who committed suicide in *Satyricon*'s backstage (DVD, Criterion Collection).
The idea that sees the actor as a puppet moved by the director through invisible threads
can be traced back to the theoretical writings of Sebastiano Arturo Luciani (1884–1950),

Lina Wertmüller's style is inscribed in this horizon of directorial simulation and preparation, but in her case, there is more: for her, the game of puppetry led to a collaboration and apprenticeship with one of the greatest international artists of puppet theater, Maria Signorelli. Little has been written about the kinship between Wertmüller's cinematic work and the puppet theater or about the multimedia nature of her career divided between theater, puppetry, radio, television, and film.[3] Taking into consideration the directorial and performative ramifications of this experience, which Wertmüller recalled as "exalting and very useful,"[4] in contact with the puppet theater and especially the sui generis theater of Signorelli, allows us to rediscover the theatricality inherent in some of Wertmüller's key films, including *Mimì metallurgico ferito nell'onore* (*The Seduction of Mimì*, 1972), *Film d'amore e anarchia, ovvero stamattina alle 10 in Via dei Fiori nella nota casa di tolleranza* (*Love and Anarchy*, 1973), and *Pasqualino Settebellezze* (*Seven Beauties*, 1975). In this way, we come to highlight the original intersection of theater and cinematography in Wertmüller's choreographic approach to directing. The choreography found in famous sequences relating to dance as well as stillness, often considered among the most original features of this director's works, spring from a special sensibility for the nonverbal language typical of the puppet theater.

a musicologist and film critic who from early in his career analyzed cinema according to a perspective akin to modern intermediality: see his article "L'idealità del cinematografo" in *In Penombra*, 2.1, January 1919, now in Claudio Camerini and Riccardo Redi, *Tra una film e l'altra: materiali sul cinema muto italiano 1907–1920* (Venice: Marsilio, 1980), 206–209.

[3] The text by Ernest Ferlita and John R. May mentions puppetry only in passing, while Masucci's biography, although rich in testimonies, excludes this phase of the director's career altogether. In her monograph, Grace Russo Bullaro acknowledges the eclectic and complex reality of Wertmüller's artistic work; however, she focuses only on cinema and in particular on the director's best-known films, created during the 1970s. See Ernest Ferlita and John R. May, *The Parables of Lina Wertmüller* (Toronto: Paulist Press, 1977); Tiziana Masucci, *I chiari di Lina*, Cantalupo in Sabina (RI), Edizioni Sabinae, 2009; Grace Russo Bullaro, *Man in Disorder. The Cinema of Lina Wertmüller in the 1970s* (Leicester, UK: Troubador Publishing, 2006), 107.

[4] Lina Wertmüller, "Maria Signorelli: una bacchetta magica," in *Maria Signorelli tra scena e libri. A life for the theater*, ed. Giancarlo Sammartano and Alessia Oteri (Kaplan: Turin, 2011), 134.

Lina Wertmüller's experience in Signorelli's company L'Opera dei Burattini is chronologically inserted between two phases: her participation as an actress from the mid-1940s in the theatrical Academy of Pietro Scharoff (1886–1966), a student of Konstantin Sergeyevich Stanislavsky (1863–1938), and an apprenticeship as a scriptwriter and assistant director for theater, television, and film that goes from the mid-1950s until 1963, when she finally assisted Fellini during the shooting of *8 ½*.[5] However, it was in the postwar period, during her intense activity as a puppeteer together with Maria Signorelli, that Wertmüller experimented with directing for the first time. As she recalls in an interview she gave to Nina Winter in the late 1970s, Lina also experienced the joys and sorrows that often accompanied those provocative performances: "Later, after the war, some of us began to work with puppets and to travel around Europe with our little theater... Children came to see us and their mothers were shocked. In Sardinia they threw tomatoes at us and the police chased us out of the villages. We caused scandals and it was always an adventure."[6] Talking to John Simon, the director pointed out that mothers were surprised because while they were expecting to see something like Cinderella, they instead found themselves in front of Picasso-like shows inspired by Kafka.[7]

As dance historian Patrizia Veroli notes, Signorelli's puppets can be associated with those of Fortunato Depero, Paul Klee, and Alexandra Ekster, and in them, one breathes the soul of the European avant-garde of the early twentieth century, from the futurist sculpture of Umberto Boccioni to the tactilism of Filippo Tommaso Marinetti and even to the coeval characters in search of an author by Luigi Pirandello (see an example in Fig. 10.1).[8] These influences have strong biographical roots

[5] L. Wertmüller, *Tutto a posto e niente in ordine* (Mondadori: Milan, 2012), 43. See E. Ferlita and J. R. May, op. cit., p. 10 and G. R. Bullaro, op. cit., pp. xiii–xv. For some biographical details regarding Wertmüller's youthful experiences in the theater, see the interview *Il cinema italiano testimonianze e protagonisti*, edited by C. Lizzani in the DVD Extras *Il cinema italiano, testimonianze e protagonisti*. Lizzani in the Extras of the DVD *The Lina Wertmüller Collection* (Koch Lorber Films, 2001).

[6] L. Wertmüller, "Lina Wertmüller," in *Interview with the Muse*, ed. N. Winter (Berkeley: Moon Books, 1978), 201.

[7] John Simon, "Wertmüller's 'Seven Beauties'—Call It a Masterpiece," *New York* IX, no. 5 (1976): 30.

[8] Patrizia Veroli, *Maria Signorelli's Puppets*, from the *Maria Signorelli Collection* website (March 2017), www.collezionemariasignorelli.it.

Fig. 10.1 A
photograph of puppets
built by Maria Signorelli
(Courtesy of Maristella
Campolunghi and
Giuseppina Valpicelli)

because Maria Signorelli spent her youth in a house where, thanks to
the intellectual vitality of her mother Olga Resnevic-Signorelli, figures
such as Pirandello, Giovanni Papini, Marinetti, the de Chirico brothers,
the Bragaglia brothers, and Giuseppe Ungaretti came to visit.[9] Maria
Signorelli collaborated as a set designer and assistant director in the Teatro
degli Indipendenti with Anton Giulio Bragaglia (1890–1960)—a photographer, art critic, director, and leading figure in the Futurist movement,
even if rejected at certain junctures by the followers of Marinetti—
and author, among other things, of the historical study on Pulcinella

[9] L. Wertmüller, *Maria Signorelli*, op. cit., p. 132.

mentioned in a previous chapter.[10] It was in fact in the Casa d'Arte Bragaglia, a symbolic place of Italian experimentation in those years, that the Roman artistic society came to know Signorelli's puppets, which were soon exhibited in shows in Florence, Berlin, and finally Paris with a presentation by Giorgio de Chirico. The words of the great painter help us understand how the avant-garde was substantially attracted by the transformative quality of Signorelli's craftsmanship, that is, by her ability to raise raw, everyday materials to a plane of high lyricism:

> Maria Signorelli—in her tragic and passionate, troubled and disquieting dolls—reveals her love for changing matter, mutating, when sewn, expression and voice. It is the rag, the scrap of cloth, the piece of wood—yes, the vile piece of wood that has escaped decay—the thread knotted into lace, the twisted or unraveled cord that, united in a bundle with other cords, its brothers, hangs like the hair of a desperate Cassandra.[11]

The transmutation of the humble into the poetic is indeed the most notable quality of Maria Signorelli's work, about which Giuseppe Ungaretti once wrote, "The power of illusion that Maria Signorelli has at her disposal must be quite extraordinary in order to give to a small piece of tulle, a fragment of string or felt, a piece of glass, a bit of fabric both plastic and lyrical effects."[12]

Signorelli's workshop attracted and trained numerous young artists (including Silvano Agosti, Carlo Verdone, and Gabriele Ferzetti). The young Lina took her place in the group of the Opera dei Burattini mainly as a choreographer—alongside Scilla Brini, Luigi Mian, and Paolo Tommasi—curating, between 1949 and 1954, numerous musical performances and ballets, including Prokofiev's *Pierino e il lupo* (*Peter and the Wolf*), Offenbach's *Can Can* (*Infernal Galop*), and Rossini's *Tarantella*; at the same time, she took her first steps as a director with fairy tales

[10] The encounter with the puppet theater was certainly influential also for his brother Carlo Ludovico Bragaglia (1894–1998), who, much more active as a director, followed the theatrical line in cinema through the man-marionette par excellence, Totò, starting with *Animali pazzi* in 1939.

[11] The quotations by de Chirico and Ungaretti come from the *Brochure di presentazione* in the Ferrari Archive at the Castello dei Burattini in Parma.

[12] Ibid., 11.

Fig. 10.2 Example of a playbill for a show by Maria Signorelli listing the collaboration with Lina Wertmüller (Courtesy of the archive of the Castello dei Burattini. Museo Giordano Ferrari of Parma)

such as *La bella addormentata nel bosco* (*Sleeping Beauty*) and *Il drago geloso* (*The Jealous Dragon*) and adaptations of classical and modern texts including Cesare Pascarella's *La scoperta dell'America* (*The Discovery of America*), Carlo Gozzi's *Il re cervo* (*The Deer King*, Fig. 10.2), and Oscar Wilde's *L'usignolo e la rosa* (*The Nightingale and the Rose*).[13]

[13] In the *Brochure di repertorio* "Opera dei burattini 1947–1957," which can be consulted in the Ferrari Archive of the Castello dei Burattini of Parma, we find evidence of

During her apprenticeship in Signorelli's company, Lina Wertmüller came into contact with a vast repertoire. Through this experience, the director undoubtedly honed her sensitivity to both the satirical elements of traditional *zanni* comedy and the lyrical potential of nonverbal language. These two inseparable areas of action, the satirical and the plastic, are the pillars of the distinctive theatrical quality of Lina Wertmüller's cinema, which hinges on a vision of the actor, and therefore of the human being, filtered through the metaphor of the puppet.

Through a concretely playful and explorative satire offered by puppet theatricality, and therefore on the basis of her experience with Signorelli, Lina Wertmüller has sought to stage the dilemma of realizing the human potential within the obstacles of social life. Wertmüller's prior experience in the theater of puppets and marionettes can be found in the deeper structure of her cinematic gaze. Her background in puppetry helps us to understand her directorial aspirations, which are dominated by the attempt to emancipate the spectators according to a personal form of existential socialism through a cinematic puppet–human dynamic. Finally, this director's background in puppetry also makes it possible to transcend the accusations of repetitiveness, boorishness, histrionics, and degradation that many Italian film historians have lamented about Wertmüller's films.[14] When considered in relation to the sensibility of puppetry, such negative traits actually exist to flag the existing proximity between puppet

Lina Wertmüller's work as choreographer in *Pupazzetti* (November 1949), *Le cigale et la fourmi* (January 1951), *Pierino e il lupo* (December 1952), *Minuetto* (December 1952), *Can Can* (May 1954 with Paolo Tommasi), and *La Tarantella* (November 1954); as director in *La bella addormentata nel bosco* (December 1950), *Il drago geloso* (December 1950), *La scoperta dell'America* (October 1951), *Il Re Cervo* (December 1952), *Il dialogo del tenente Colonnello della Guardia Civile* (December 1952 with Paolo Tommasi), and *L'usignolo e la rosa* (December 1952); and in a few cases also as a puppeteer actress and text editor.

[14] Lino Miccichè's opinion is the most abrasive: "We acknowledge Lina Wertmüller's merit of coherence: her cinema degrades more and more, from film to film, with a constant progression." Gian Piero Brunetta, although recording the positive aspects, underlines the limitations of a "contrived formula" that "once it has reached full mastery of the professional means" has "no measure of equilibrium, juxtaposing drama and melodrama, social denunciation and apathy, reality and fable." In the opinion of another eminent Italian critic, Paolo Mereghetti, the "boorishness," the "too-numerous histrionic stances" and the "taste for excess and caricature" are identified as factors that devalue Wertmüller's work and its worth, whether it be artistic, political, or existential. See Lino Miccichè, *Cinema italiano degli anni settanta* (Venice: Marsilio, 1980), 212; Gian Piero Brunetta, *Storia del cinema italiano dal 1945 agli anni ottanta* (Rome: Editori Riuniti, 1982), 708;

and actor, between film and street farce, and between the director's gaze and the puppeteer's eye.

The same operation of marginalization carried out by high-brow Italian criticism against Wertmüller is very similar to the one that practitioners of commedia dell'arte and then also puppeteers had to endure at various points of history; they were accused of corrupting, with their fatuity and vulgarity, the tastes and morals of the spectators.[15] It is not by chance that puppets, historical heirs to the fortunes and misfortunes of the commedia dell'arte, find their strength precisely in being an irreparably popular form of art, always on the margins and always in conflict with the customs of the *benpensanti*, the conformist sector of society.[16] Even Wertmüller's rebellious and demystifying impertinence, her ability to stand reinvigorated at the blows of the critical ax, can be traced back to her artistic genesis in puppetry.

As is well known, the satire of Wertmüller's cinema focuses on political and moral hypocrisy and on humankind's claims to rationality and objectivity. According to the classic comic theme of love madness, man and woman are represented in her films in the grip of sexual impulses, to which the principles of politics and morality are subordinated. The contrast between compelling needs and moral positions—or as one of the fathers of modern satirical comedy, Niccolò Machiavelli, put it, between how one lives and how one should live—is another variant of the friction between sexuality and politics, a dominant theme in Wertmüller's work. From *Travolti da un insolito destino nell'azzurro mare d'agosto* (*Swept Away*, 1974) to *Metalmeccanico e parrucchiera presi da un vortice di politica e di sesso* (*The Blue Collar Worker and the Hairdresser in a Whirl of Politics and Sex*, 1996), the male protagonist betrays his leftist ideology by losing his head to a woman from the opposite political side and eventually becoming submissive to her (serpentine titles such as those above are but another reminder of the Renaissance *canovacci*). In this latter film there are even explicit references to the division of the protagonist into

Paolo Mereghetti and Alberto Pezzotta, *Il Mereghetti: dizionario dei film 2006* (Milan: Baldini Castoldi Dalai, 2005), 997, 1633.

[15] On the other hand, Brunetta himself correctly intuits Wertmüller's power in her being "a popular storyteller of Italian cinema" and the reasons for her success in "a folk memory that has never completely disappeared." G. P. Brunetta, *Storia del cinema*, op. cit., p. 708.

[16] Cf. F. Pacchioni, *La passione di un Burattino*, op. cit.

two parts: "from the waist up on the left and from the waist down on the right," recalling figures of satyr and centaur.[17]

While the satire of reason belongs to a broader comic tradition and not only to puppet theater, it is the implicit intermedial references, linked to the choreographic aspects, that bear the strongest witness to the shadow of the puppet-marionette in Wertmüller's films. There is a particular way in which Wertmüller presents social typologies by grouping them clearly and placing them in contrast with each other, like the bodies of a ballet of figures placed to occupy the predetermined and restricted corner of a small stage. For example, in *Mimì metallurgico ferito nell'onore*, Sicilian workers who have emigrated to the North are crowded into a corner of the frame and presented in opposition to the small group of mafiosi who try to control and exploit them. This choreographic perspective, in which actors and the objects are equivalent to puppets that move according to the rhythmic logic of a *bambocciata*, is manifested in the numerous ballets staged in Wertmüller's films. The most evident case belongs to *Film d'amore e d'anarchia*, where the dancing energy of the prostitutes of the Roman brothel always seems to be on the verge of breaking into a musical. And when the actors move in this way, their figures placed in symmetrical lines and the movements of their legs evoke the can-can ballets that the young Lina directed in Signorelli's little theater. In another memorable sequence, this time from *Paqualino Settebellezze*, the dance imagined by the protagonist recalls puppet theater, and the appearance of a woman-marionette evokes the archetype of the female body as a self-propelled statue endowed with divinatory abilities.

Wertmüller's theatrical forma mentis is revealed in the musical sequences where gestures and choreography replace dialogue and speech. A famous example is in *Mimì metallurgico*: the declaration of love, all gestural, addressed by Carmelo (Giancarlo Giannini) to Fiorella (Mari-angela Melato), generates an alternation of surrendering and refusal, of emotional blackmail and platonic love. Another admirable sequence is undoubtedly the dialogue made entirely of glances between Tunin (Gian-carlo Giannini), Salome (Mariangela Melato), and Tripolina (Lina Polito) in *Film d'amore e d'anarchia*, conveying passion, curiosity, fear, falling

---

[17] Another typical element of Italian comic-satirical tradition is the marked regionality of the characters: a recurring characteristic in almost all of Wertmüller's films is, in fact, the overemphasis on typically local accents and expressions and the clash among characters of different origins.

in love, jealousy, and resignation. Or again, in this same film, another example comprises the tender manifestations of complicity between Tunin and his old anarchist mentor who, after flashback scenes where he is observed making the theatrical leaps of an irreverent puppet, is seen hanging lifeless from a tree along the river, recalling the end of the protagonist of the novel *La testa di Alvise* (*The Head of Alvise* by Wertmüller), who also dies hanging from a tree like a "broken puppet."[18] Such sequences, where the puppet-like dimension of the actor and the very careful arrangement of movements and gestures dominate the frame, rank among the highest peaks of Wertmüller's cinema. Choreography is also joined by makeup, which undoubtedly recalls the faces of Maria Signorelli's puppets, strongly expressive in their rough and messy materiality.

It is also interesting to note how, despite the greater closeness between string puppet and actor in the movement of the limbs, Wertmüller prefers *burattini* controlled from below, finding them "more human" and "more Italian thanks to the movement of the hands."[19] The *burattino*, though legless and less realistic than the *marionetta*, generally appears as more human precisely because of the fluid and organic motion of the hand that guides it from within, which is very different from the abstract mechanicalness of the strings that move the marionette. The fluidity and humanity of the puppet, however, contrast with an appearance that is only approximately human, giving rise to an effect of parody instead of the sense of wonder of the verisimilar and magical puppet. Faithful to her satirical intentions, Wertmüller cannot but prefer the *burattino* to the *marionetta*, and therefore she highlights in her actors the same immediate and organic gestural expressiveness, the same rebellious and ridiculous force: the human who makes fun of humans. The conceptual interest in the glove puppet, however, is mixed with the unequivocal presence of the marionette, linked to the apprenticeship with Signorelli and to the actor's body, justifying the identification of a puppet-marionette underlying the theatrical-cinematic aesthetics of this director.

We are able to understand how, in the sequences highlighted above, such an original and powerful aesthetic is given by the intersection

---

[18] L. Wermüller, *Essere o avere. Ma per essere devo avere LA TESTA DI ALVISE su un piatto d'argento* (Milan: Rizzoli, 1981), 216–217.

[19] The quote is contained in J. Simon, op. cit., p. 30.

of different arts, that of puppet theater and that of cinema. Aesthetic innovation soars in these moments, especially because intermediality here supports the deep message of the films which, as we mentioned before, intends to communicate the tragicomic human condition of being figuratively *in the hands of* our own irrational nature. In such purely choreographic and gestural sequences, in which characters show themselves for the puppets they are, the circle comes to a close; in those moments, we understand their very human and ridiculous tragedy of unaware automata, and, at the same time, we enjoy their superhuman grace and innocence. This elevation from the vile to the lyrical brings us back to the distinctive feature of the dolls built by Maria Signorelli, which Giorgio de Chirico and Giuseppe Ungaretti celebrated precisely for the change from the coarse to the poetic, for the "escape from rottenness," according to the hermetic poet. The shadow of the puppet transpires in some of Wertmüller's films through a certain compassionate satire, but it also enters as a spiritualizing agent of romantic memory. Emphasizing the puppet-like dimension of the actor therefore leads not only into the sphere of the comical but also toward a spiritual perspective of reality that appears as the only way to redeem the often crude and boorish humanity of the characters. The puppet domain, on a metaphorical level, seems to be the expressive key toward which Wertmüller's films yearn, the way to miraculously raise characters who would otherwise be doomed to degradation and vulgarity.[20]

In virtue of the relationship that, for Wertmüller, exists between her work in directing and puppetry, it is appropriate to return once again to Maria Signorelli, though this time linking to the latter's pedagogical activity. In the wake of the ideas of her husband, the educator Luigi

---

[20] It is also no coincidence that Lina Wertmüller was fond of the work of Guido Ceronetti (1927–2018), an eclectic and still largely unknown figure of the Italian twentieth century who combined a very active and fascinating career as a puppeteer to philosophical and literary research on the modern condition. Lina Wertmüller expressed her interest and affinity with Ceronetti by commenting on a page of *La carta è stanca* (*Paper is Tired*, 1976), see: E. Ferlita and J. R. May, op. cit., pp. 85–86. Almost at the same time as Wertmüller, Ceronetti approached cinema in the early 1960s, composing numerous subjects that were strongly critical of the social trends that the economic boom was producing in Italy, in particular on themes such as the marginalization of the subject in the urban context and the exploitation of human and natural resources caused by growing consumerism. See Stefano Stoja, *Il cinema di Guido Ceronetti: Tu vuo' fa' l'Americano...*, "Cartevive", Periodico dell'Archivio Prezzolini, Biblioteca cantonale Lugano, 2009, pp. 79–99.

Volpicelli (1900–1983), Signorelli wrote about the psychosocial formative value of puppet play, describing it as an "act of knowledge" and as an
education in the "rebellious matter" of the "game of life."[21] Similarly, the
grotesque game of Wertmüller's films, with its puppet-like choreography,
its masks, and the superimposition of the puppet-marionette on the actor,
generates a reflexive distance that is nothing other than the cognitive act
of which Signorelli speaks. It is a distance due to the theatrical device that
stages the bubbling up of the rebellious matter of life and highlights the
gap between the ideals of freedom and rationality and biopolitical forces.
The gap between self and acting, between nature and culture, between
will and duty, between individual and society, of which the puppet is
emblem and instrument, allows Wertmüller to satirize humanity and, in
this way, make it known. Lina Wertmüller narrates how the individual
tries to find him or herself in the chaos of existence, in an intermediate
position between order and disorder; the director's attempt to capture
this process of understanding and self-acceptance often succeeds thanks
to the puppet.[22]

[21] Maria Signorelli, *L'esperienza scolastica del teatro* (Rome: Armando Editore, 1963),
16, 20.

[22] In summarizing the director's ideology, Ferlita and May write, "Wertmüller's
socialism is not identified with 'the proletarian masses;' it is a socialism that at its root is
concerned with individual freedom.... Her films could not be clearer or more consistent
in portraying the deplorable systems that stifle freedom" (E. Ferlita and J. R. May, op.
cit., p. 11).

CHAPTER 11

The Emigrated *Pupo*: Ritualism and Italian American Identity

Abstract This chapter traces the transfer of the southern Italian *opera dei pupi* to North America in its impact on avant-garde theater—especially in the case of Remo Bufano—and its function in terms of generational and identity dynamics. Owing to its rigidity and its Ariostesque repertoire, the pupo allows for a blending of myth and history, which is utilized in creative ways, especially in independent and experimental filmmaking. This is shown in the film *Tarantella* by Helen de Michiel. However, the *opera dei pupi* is also a significant cultural marker in Hollywood mafia films, such as in Coppola's *The Godfather* trilogy, and it provides a reservoir of innovative acting styles for performers such as John Turturro.

Keywords Puppets · Italian puppetry · Italian cinema · Don Quixote · Opera dei pupi · Sicily · Ariosto · Remo Bufano · Helen de Michiel · John Turturro · Mimmo Cuticchio · Identity · History · Myth · Female perspective

While in the more rarefied case of Pasolini's *pupo*, the puppet theater is embraced in its totality, employing the metaphor of the puppet to convey broader existential views; in the Rossellinian case, the potential of historical understanding inherent in the *pupo* is revealed alongside this puppet's cross-cultural role. The transnational function of the Italian

F. Pacchioni, *The Image of the Puppet in Italian Theater,
Literature and Film*, https://doi.org/10.1007/978-3-030-98668-1_11

puppet theater can be traced within the context of independent Italian American cinema, where the *pupo* stands out for its strong predisposition toward identity discourse.

Historians have pointed out that one of the main reasons why the *opera dei pupi* established itself as the main form of puppet theater in southern Italy in the eighteenth and nineteenth centuries was the "strong emotional charge that characterizes the relationship between the character of the *opra* and the public" and the "mythical function" that the *pupi*'s vicissitudes assumed within the popular worldview.[1] The culturally homogeneous public, formed mostly by males belonging to subordinate classes (peasants, artisans, and proletarians), found in the cycle of representations a ritual of belonging where themes such as struggle, survival, friendship, hatred, and betrayal were codified and at the same time transported into the sphere of myth.[2]

The function performed by the *pupo* in Italian American cinema does not detach itself from the ritualistic quality proper to this form of theater; on the contrary, it confirms it for the purpose of recovering and safeguarding a cultural history of origin. This means that, in recent times, the *pupo* has continued to live on in the Italian American imagination, serving as an instrument to forge a new bond between America and Italy. One of the peculiarities of the metaphorical value of the *pupo* that can be found in the American context is its manifestation within artistic works marked by independent modes of production. In these cases, in an attempt to break free from the limitations of the commercial schemes of Italian American-themed films, a line of continuity is observed that connects the cinema to both the work of Italian immigrant puppeteers and to American avant-garde theater.

European migrants brought their traditions of popular theater with them across the ocean. The first puppeteers to land on the American continent were Spanish, following the expedition of Hernán Cortés in the early sixteenth century, followed by the English, who established the glove

---

[1] Antonio Buttitta, "L'opera dei pupi come rito," in AA.VV., *I pupi e il teatro*, monographic number of "Quaderni di teatro", IV, 13, 1981, p. 33. For an overview on the opera dei pupi, see also Jo Ann Cavallo, "Sicilian Puppet Theater," in *The Literary Encyclopedia*, 16 January 2012. http://www.litencyc.com/php/stopics.php?rec=true&UID=17676, accessed 1 May 2019.

[2] Ibid., pp. 31–32. See also Antonio Pasqualino and Janne Vibaek, "Registri linguistici e linguaggi non verbali nell'opera dei pupi," in *Semiotica della rappresentazione*, ed. Renato Tomasino (Palermo: Flaccovio, 1984), 109–115.

puppet tradition along the East Coast during the eighteenth century.[3] The first appearances of Italian puppeteers were recorded in the early nineteenth century, when Italian immigration was beginning to grow. In the early twentieth century, in a small theater on Mulberry Street, the Sicilian Manteo family, one of the most renowned puppeteering families, staged an episode of *Orlando Furioso* every night, taking, as usual, more than a year to complete the cycle.[4] The Sicilian American community continued to appreciate this form of entertainment, favoring its maintenance as a ritual of belonging.

The *pupo* had a particular vitality in North America, influencing even the domains of experimental theater. Indeed, the Sicilian exodus of those years coincided with the development of influential avant-garde perspectives in stage theater inspired by puppetry, particularly the call to move beyond naturalism by British actor Edward Gordon Craig. Craig's bold 1907 manifesto, *The Actor and the Uber-Marionette*, identifies the puppet, thanks to its capacity of increasing the symbolic and expressive value of performance, as one of the primary tools for the renewal of Western theater.[5] In the multicultural heart of New York City, puppet theater contributed to the development of modern American theater through a number of young puppeteers who knew how to combine tradition and experimentation, as demonstrated by the fascinating case of Remo Bufano (1894–1948), who transported the Sicilian American puppets of Mulberry Street into the international theatrical avant-garde.

Bufano, who moved with his family to New York City at an early age, grew up in the shadow of the Manteo family's shows and exhibited a strong interest in the construction and manipulation of puppets from a young age. Working in various stable, itinerant, traditional, and experimental contexts, Bufano collaborated with the famous symbolist theater company Provincetown Playhouse, inspired by Craig's ideas (his sets with masks, animated objects, and puppets for *Vote the New Moon: A Toy Play* of 1920 are worthy of mention). Bufano then played a central role in the

[3] Paul McPharlin, *The Puppet Theater in America: A History 1524–1948* (Boston: Plays Inc., 1949), 6, 7 and 37.

[4] John Bell, *American Puppet Modernism: Essays on the Material World in Performance* (New York: Palgrave, 2008), 75.

[5] Edward Gordon Craig, *Craig on Theater*, edited by J. Michael Walton (London: Methuen, 1983), 82–86 (First edition: "The Actor and the über-marionette," in *The Mask*, Vols. 1 and 2, Florence, 1908).

international success of Spanish composer Manuel de Falla's play *Retablo de Maese Pedro*, presented in 1925 and centered on the well-known scene from *Don Quixote* in which, we recall, the knight-errant attends Master Puppeteer Pedro's show where a princess is kidnapped by soldiers; mistaking the play for a real event, Don Quixote intervenes by destroying the marionettes. To highlight and expand the discourse on representation and reality at the heart of Cervantes' text, Bufano drew on his knowledge of puppetry in an extremely original way, staging all the characters—the princess, the soldiers, Mastro Pedro, and Don Quixote himself—with large *pupi* of various sizes manipulated with the help of assistants. Remo Bufano was also responsible for staging puppets for Brock Pemberton's melodrama *Puppets* (also titled *The Marionette Man* and *The Knife in the Wall*, 1925), in which an Italian puppeteer is drafted into the army during World War I and, upon return, eventually discovers that his loved one has betrayed him. The play was adapted into a film titled *Puppets* (1926), directed by George Archimbaud, which is now considered a lost film. According to reviews of the time, the film depicted the dwelling and theater of the Italian puppeteer.[6]

Most of the contact between puppets and cinema in the first half of the twentieth century occurred in Europe, especially within expressionist and impressionist cinematic currents. In classical Hollywood cinema, such contact occurred much less, due to the dominating interest in perfecting narrative continuity rather than exploring abstraction. The case of *I Am Suzanne!*, featuring the collaboration with Podrecca, and analyzed in a previous chapter, was certainly an exception; furthermore in this film, the marionettes increased the aura of danger and madness surrounding the relationship between Suzanne and the puppeteer Tony. Interestingly, the *pupi* resurface within the gangster genre to evoke the sense of primitive violence perceived as inherent in Sicilian culture, which increases the tragic and mythical tone of this genre. Take, for example, the famous scene of the stalking and killing of Don Fannucci (Gastone Moschin) by the young Vito Corleone (Robert De Niro) in Coppola's *The Godfather Part II*, when Vito follows his victim with a feline step from the rooftops of Little Italy, while in the street the feast of San Gennaro and a *pupi* show are taking place (staged by the Manteo family). In the crosscutting of this famous sequence, the puppets' struggle parallels Vito Corleone's

[6] J. Bell, op. cit., pp. 71–81.

charge of violence and evokes the idea of ancient feuds and desires for revenge. The *pupi* as expression of archaic violence return in *Godfather Part III* (Francis Ford Coppola, 1990), this time as a counterpoint to Michael Corleone (Al Pacino) failing attempt to restore his ex-wife Kay's trust in him as a family man (Diane Keaton). While Michael is showing Kay the town of Corleone, they bump into a wedding celebration which leads Kay to reveal to Michael that their daughter is in love with an Italian man, a news to which Michael immediately disapproves in line with his old-world paternal authority. In the following scene, they stop in front of a *pupi* performance, where a Count is punishing his daughter with death for having had a secret affair with her cousin (paralleling the forbidden and lethal love affairs between Michael daughter Sofia and her cousin Vincent). At the cruel spectacle, Kay makes a sneering remark meant to point out to her ex-husband the hypocritical and destructive traits of Sicilian "honor." It must be noted that this sequence features Mimmo Cuticchio (1948–), perhaps the most prominent Italian *puparo*, in the role of *cuntista* (oral storyteller) narrating the events around the puppet show while brandishing a sword as according to tradition.

Subsequently, Italian American filmmakers have effectively turned to *l'opera dei pupi* as a stylistic source in an attempt to create a new ethnic image on the big screen and a cinematic identity of their own. The examples of *Tarantella*, directed by Helen De Michiel in 1995, and *Rehearsal for a Sicilian Tragedy*, a 2009 documentary created by Roman Paska and John Turturro, offer clear evidence of the way that Sicilian *pupi* and cinema have intersected in order to reveal a new Sicilian and more generally Italian identity in the United States.

Tarantella, the debut feature by director Helen De Michiel (1953–), is the story of Diane (Mira Sorvino), a young photographer who, upon hearing the news of her mother's death, returns to her childhood home after a long absence. Centering on the story of the women in Diane's family, *Tarantella* is a rare example of an attempt to recover the female perspective of Italian American immigration. With the help of an old friend, Diane reads in her mother's diary the dramatic story of her grandmother, who fled the country of her birth after poisoning her violent husband. As Diane proceeds to read the diary, past events are shown through the device of a *pupi* show, the same *pupi* that Diane later finds among her mother's possessions and decides to take with her at the end of the film. Among the various fantasies of the protagonist that contribute to giving the film its considerable narrative depth, the *pupi* show is the most extensive and significant. As it has been noted, the *pupi* show functions in *Tarantella*, in a manner analogous to culinary recipes, as an instrument of recollection and, simultaneously, as an ethnic-artistic *bildungsroman*.[7]

Showing past events of the plot, which take place in Calabria, through a *pupi* show instead of flashbacks with real actors was certainly a good solution for this limited-fund, independent production. The sensibility of the Italian American director De Michiel is combined with her attendance at the shows of the Heart of the Beast Puppet and Mask Theatre in Minneapolis under the direction of Sandra Spieler, where De Michiel had seen shows with poignant atmospheres linked to various themes of social justice. Working with Sandra Spieler, Helen De Michiel designed a series of scenes with *pupi*, elaborated and enriched thanks to the research that the director had carried out in Calabria, photographing faces and recording traditions. In an interview I conducted with the director, De Michiel lucidly described the aesthetic reasons behind the choice of puppets.

> My research in Calabria convinced me that puppetry would link the past with the present, the ancestors with the current realities, the memories with the history of these women. I wanted to evoke a sense of time-out-of-time and dig into their emotional realities through these non-human entities. Plus, the story was so distant and furtive, using puppets made it actually seem plausible in a counter-intuitive way.[8]

Echoing the modernist theatrical sensibility of Bontempelli, the *pupo* opens the doors to a distinctly poetic and symbolic representation, aimed at evoking a mythical past beyond history. This particular poetic value reveals the transmedial vitality of the repertoire specific to this type of popular theater, where historiography and imagination are mixed according to Ariosto's methods. In *Tarantella*, the scenes with the *pupi* relate directly to the fantastic reconstruction of the family history that takes place in Diane's mind.

The symbiotic relationship between the two arts develops through an exchange that influences the film on various aesthetic levels. For example, the reduced plasticity typical of the *pupi*, operated by one metal bar at the

---

[7] John Paul Russo, "Director's Cut: Italian Americans Filming Italian Americans," in *Mediated Ethnicity: New American Cinema*, a cura di Giuliana Muscio (New York: Calandra Italian American Institute, 2010), 152–153.

[8] The quote comes from an unpublished interview occurred on March 11, 2012.

Fig. 11.1 Screenshot from *Tarantella* (dir. Helen de Michiel, 1995), DVD

head and another at the hand, expresses the static nature of the figures of Diane's family's past, who she must learn to accept for who they are. Even the gory characteristics of *pupi* theatricality—where we traditionally see severed heads and limbs, eyes poking out, and bodies split in half—are cleverly used in the film, giving life to an overall adventurous and tragic narrative, but also giving rise to particularly touching scenes, such as the one in which the grandmother's *pupo* removes its face, showing another face marked by the secret of a monstrous pain (Fig. 11.1).

The search for an Italian American aesthetic in cinema also led John Turturro (1957–) to delve into the mine of the *opera dei pupi*, this time the Palermo one, which, among other unique characteristics, also presents the manipulation of the *pupo* from the sides of the scene, thus reinforcing in a certain way the transfer between the *pupo* and the *puparo* (the *pupi* puppeteer) as actor. *Rehearsal for a Sicilian Tragedy* is a diary film that collects notes for a future film about the sorrowful love story of a Sicilian puppeteer. As a guide in his research, Turturro chose puppeteer extraordinaire Mimmo Cuticchio, already mentioned in connection to Coppola's generational mafia masterpiece.

Turturro's case, too, exemplifies a search for artistic roots, as is made clear in the scene of the director's return to his mother's house and during the dialogue with the *puparo's* son, Giacomo Cuticchio, who explains his total dedication to the family tradition. The relationship between father and son embodies the continuity between traditional identity and artistic vocation that Turturro had already highlighted in his directorial debut, *Mac*, in 1992. Turturro dedicated the film to his father, a bricklayer, who defended the artisanal and skillful quality of his work against the laws of business: this is the basis of an authentically and revolutionarily Italian American path of moral and artistic knowledge.

The theater has taken on increasing importance in Turturro's cinema; one need only think of the comic-philosophical vicissitudes of the company of theater actors in *Illuminata* (1995) and the New York musical drama *Romance and Cigarettes* (2005, a film that then led Turturro in 2010 to explore the Neapolitan musical scene in *Passione*). In his roles, Turturro delivers a theatrical performance, aimed at a hyper-dramatic, sometimes grotesque quality. In both *Mac* and his other films, Turturro seems to model himself on the character of a crazed Orlando, modernly obsessed with the quest for a fulfillment that is at once aesthetic, cultural, and ideological.

Rehearsal for a Sicilian Tragedy definitively clarifies the relationship Turturro seeks between cinema and theater, between craft and art, and between America and Italy. The *pupo* as a model for acting unites all these levels. In the film, Turturro approaches the specific techniques of the *puparo* as a way to give new vigor and a Sicilian flavor to his performance. There are sequences where the actor tries to master the acting methods and the breath of the *puparo*—in particular, the technique of the *lamentu*, the vibration of the voice to communicate drama—and where he shares the stage with the *pupo* imitating his gestures. One may like to imagine, together with Turturro, his future film based on the notes he collected, where he will perhaps split into the character of the *puparo* and the *pupo* itself.

Finally, this return to the transmedial application of the *pupo* in cinema, along the lines of historical and meta-historical reflection, is to be considered an exquisitely Italian American reinterpretation of an element that we had already noted in the Italian cinematic tradition. In this return through Italian American screens, the *pupo* continues to serve as a tool to explore and express the folds of Italian identity, straddling distant geographical and temporal dimensions. The Sicilian puppet brings with it the ability to reconnect with the island's past, identity, and artistic vocation. Just like *opera dei pupi* metabolized a history of foreign invasion for the inhabitants of Sicily, this type of puppetry is revealed to be today, in these cinematic texts, a device for the preservation and reinterpretation of identity.

CHAPTER 12

Conclusions

Abstract The concluding chapter highlights the puppet's expressive vitality and significance as idea and image. This chapter summarizes the philosophical, cultural, and aesthetic influence that the Italian puppet theater holds across different types of media production, including digital animation. Therefore, the future of the various forms of this ancient Italian tradition is located along the thematic threads studied throughout the book, which relate to existential and political satire, the negotiation of power dynamics, the exploration of metaphysical and ecological questions, and allegorical representations of ethnic identity and history.

Keywords Pinocchio · Italian puppet theater · Italian puppetry · Burattino · Marionetta · Pupo · Pulcinella · Twentieth century · Italian literature and cinema · Digital animation · Tradition · Innovation

It is clear now, at the end of this book, that without the material power of the puppet object and the vitality that the puppet theater has had over the centuries, the metaphor of the puppet would never have been expressed with the weight and resonance that it has had and continues to have. Even in the case of Pinocchio, the most famous Italian puppet in the world, it is precisely on the theatrical referent, his wooden body, that the character's appeal is based; this is made evident by the numerous film

F. Pacchioni, *The Image of the Puppet in Italian Theater, Literature and Film*, https://doi.org/10.1007/978-3-030-98668-1_12

adaptations of this story. Let's compare, for example, the success of Luigi Comencini's television series (*Le avventure di Pinocchio*, 1972) to the critical flop of Roberto Benigni's film (*Pinocchio*, 2002). We see that the first case is characterized by a remarkable fidelity to the reality of the puppet, while the second tends to lack the extraordinary nature of Collodi's character and dissolve Pinocchio into an all too human and familiar being. The world of puppet theater bursts strongly into Comencini's series, giving it veracity and representative power: the actor is replaced by an actual puppet on several occasions, Pinocchio's bodily transformations are conveyed dramatically, and Pinocchio's arrival at Mangiafuoco's theater is the occasion for a real puppet show by the Colla family of Milan. Similarly, a director like Matteo Garrone, whose innovative talent lies precisely in both skillful management of the relationship between theatricality and reality and a keen sensitivity to the inflections and meanings of corporality, has closely researched the world of nineteenth-century theater and performance and has expressed the woodenness of his Pinocchio as much as possible through theatrical and digital effects (*Pinocchio*, 2019).

The mythical fable of Pinocchio draws its origin and strength from the popular and universal value of the tradition of the puppet theater; however, it is the lesser-known cases that, when analyzed, allow us to confirm the extension of the macroscopic characteristics of the Italian metaphor of the puppet. The interpretations of individual films such as *I bambini ci guardano* and *Nocevento* have shown how the idea of the glove puppet, which has its roots in the connotations of the ancient comedy of the *zanni*, expresses its predisposition to highlight the minority point of view and social injustice. In the same vein, the animated object in a film such as *La guerra e il sogno di Momi* also allows for the development of a critique of war by delving into childhood subjectivity.

Because of its profound ontological and epistemological value, that is, as a tool for relating to the reality of the self, the puppet—or the artistic interpretation of it—acquires particular relevance in the examination of an author's poetics, regardless of the medium in question. The chapters of this volume have shed light on the function that the puppet—and, in particular, the marionette, in its various primitive, mechanical, and magical modes—plays in the work of artists such as Marinetti, de Chirico, Bontempelli, Pirandello, Pasolini, and Wertmüller. In this way, a *fil rouge* has emerged from the modernist and avant-garde cultural tradition of the early twentieth century, where puppetry expresses a need for a higher level of freedom and human fulfillment.

We have therefore traced the evolution of a theme that can be extended well beyond the national borders of Italy. The claustrophobic fatalism of the reified universe of Tim Burton, the heartbreaking and surgical existential search of Jan Švankmajer's work, the tragicomedy of the attempted overcoming of the limits of personality and human nature explored by Spike Jonze and Charlie Kaufman, represent the metaphor of the puppet as an essential principle of thought and style.

Following the theme of the puppet has also brought together rather heterogeneous artists. The case of Pasolini and his *Cosa sono le nuvole?*, which we contrasted with the positions of Bontempelli, Bertolucci, and Rossellini, lends itself to a series of meaningful reflections on the relationship between politics and poetry. Focusing on the dynamics of remediation, Pasolini's film and Rossellini's *Paisà* demonstrate how the reinterpretation and overcoming of the traditional theatrical medium of the *opera dei pupi* allow for the expression of the search for truth, both historical and existential. These examples extend and complete the essence of the puppet theater: its predisposition to dig into the relationship between subject and history, fantasy, and social reality, while seeking (and claiming) in the cinema a higher level of truth.

In its various forms, the puppet continues to offer the perspective we need to observe the relationship between us and the forces greater than ourselves—to enter into the heart of spiritual and political questions and see beyond the illusions of history. The impetus of Italian American artists toward these forms of performance as well as the growing popularity of the puppet metaphor in mass culture are clear signs of the cultural and critical relevance of the puppet theater and of its large and influential Italian chapter.

Although technical innovations will present increasingly effective and sophisticated ways of blending actor performance with the animated object, the phenomenon of the uncanny remains an important factor in tracing the boundaries of the intermedial politics governing the relationship between puppet theater and cinema. At the same time, the need to accentuate the sensory presence of the animated character and its tactile depth, for purposes ranging from wonder to fear to satire, continues to draw film and digital artists toward the world of puppetry. In this context, Italy, as one of puppetry's main artistic homelands, can continue to provide a fertile ground for performative as well as digital artists through the richness of its theatrical traditions.

At the end of this work, the trunk I found in my father's study on that distant return to Italy is filled with new presences. The rough and heavy puppets have given way to light fantasies that, quivering in their fresh and iridescent bodies, gaze fearlessly upon the new stages that the present moment places before them.

Although artistic and personal work will always be of greater cultural value than an academic description of the facts, this study is nourished by the hope of increasing awareness of these traditions by demonstrating how much puppets and marionettes have been able to express and signify during the twentieth century and by pointing out their continued relevance and strength across media. My probing of the intermedial life of the Italian puppet theater is naturally motivated by the hope of glimpsing the future of this wonderful artistic tradition of the peninsula.

One may object that the notions of intermedial reference and the politics of remediation—revealing relationships between puppet theater and the arts—may in fact be circumscribed to the twentieth-century experiences of the writers and directors who were exposed to the performances. Such subjectivity, which, motivates and colors my own critical perspective, would therefore seem to reduce the possibility of the survival of *pupi*, *marionette*, and *burattini* in the national culture and beyond. However, it is precisely in this conjunction of critical subjectivity and cultural transformations that we observe the building of a future for this artistic phenomenon. The love for tradition, and the resulting ability to trace its influences, contributes to the institutionalization of a new abstract object. In this case, this is the simulacrum of the puppet, the image which offers itself—more portable and flexible—as an aesthetic and poetic instrument applicable to various media across a wide temporal horizon. It is the essential evocative characteristics, identified and described in the chapters of this book, that open up possibilities for the future of the Italian tradition: the satirical charge of the stylized humanity of the glove puppet, whether in the caricatural traits of the great wooden heads of the Po Valley or in the more insurrectional features of the masked smaller head of Pulcinella; the evocativeness of the marvelous and perturbing grace of the marionette, where the threads lead to revealing physical and metaphysical ecologies; or the cadaveric officiousness of the *pupo*, which lays bare the representations of identity and history.

INDEX

Note: Page numbers followed by 'n' represents footnote.

F. Pacchioni, *The Image of the Puppet in Italian Theater,
Literature and Film*, https://doi.org/10.1007/978-3-030-98668-1

124   INDEX